THEY DARED TO LIVE

THEY DARED TO LIVE

ROBERT MERRILL BARTLETT

Essay Index Reprint Series

BOOKS FOR LIBRARIES PRESS
FREEPORT, NEW YORK

First Published 1937
Reprinted 1969

STANDARD BOOK NUMBER:
8369-1273-X

LIBRARY OF CONGRESS CATALOG CARD NUMBER:
76-90606

PRINTED IN THE UNITED STATES OF AMERICA

TO
SUSAN JANE

PREFACE

In an epoch of disillusionment and despair it is heartening to consider the men and women of our modern world who have dared to live with heroism and have made life triumphant.

It is *not* true that the giants are dead! Contemporary civilization still produces individuals of noble proportions who can meet their problems victoriously and move millions of their fellow beings in ways of constructive achievement. Dictators may appear to flourish, but their influence cannot be as enduring as those who build on the foundations of reason and brotherhood.

This book introduces thirty-five of these representative personalities from thirteen nations. They come from various fields: politics, science, exploration, business, literature, art, medicine, law, education, philosophy, religion, and social reform.

They are all pioneers in their realm of effort, trail-blazers and torch-bearers. They have probed to the root of reality, matched their strength against entrenched evils, and made individual existence and humanity's struggle a happier and freer adventure.

May the inspiration of their effort make us conscious of our powers that we, too, may dare to live!

R. M. B.

CONTENTS

PREFACE

I

THEY LIVED DANGEROUSLY

1. For Humanity:
HIDEYO NOGUCHI   I

2. The Long, Hard Trail:
FRIDTJOF NANSEN   4

3. When Dreams Come True:
MARTHA BERRY   7

4. For Human Liberty:
ALBERT EINSTEIN   10

5. Redeemer of the Underworld:
THOMAS MOTT OSBORNE   13

6. "Truth Is the Country of the Free Man":
ROMAIN ROLLAND   18

7. "Playing a Good Part in a Great Scheme":
EDWARD A. WILSON   22

8. Fraternity:
EUGENE VICTOR DEBS   27

9. "She Stuck to Hull House All Her Life":
JANE ADDAMS   31

10. "Life Is Painting a Picture, Not Doing a Sum":
JUSTICE OLIVER WENDELL HOLMES   34

II

THEY BLAZED NEW TRAILS

1. A Sensitive Conscience:
JOHN GALSWORTHY   39

2. "Bitter the Chast'ning Rod":
JAMES WELDON JOHNSON   42

3. Spirit versus Force:
STEFAN ZWEIG   46

4. Friend of the Lowly:
CHARLES F. ANDREWS   50

5. A Cup of Cold Water:
MOTOICHIRO TAKAHASHI   53

6. Captain of the Pick-and-Shovel Brigade:
PIERRE CERESOLE   56

7. Awakener of Millions:
HU SHIH   59

8. He Could Not Forget the Underdog:
ANTHONY ASHLEY COOPER, LORD SHAFTESBURY   62

9. "Power to Act Is Duty to Act":
PETER KROPOTKIN   67

10. Blue Prints for a Better World:
HERBERT GEORGE WELLS   71

III

THEY CONQUERED OBSTACLES

1. Two Selves Who Became One:
ANNE SULLIVAN MACY AND HELEN KELLER   76

x

2. *"Remember Who You Are"*:
    ROLAND HAYES   80

3. *"Truth Will Prevail"*:
    TOMAS G. MASARYK   84

4. *"The Wise Man Learns to Live"*:
    CHARLES PROTEUS STEINMETZ   87

5. *"I Would Not Exchange My Suffering for the Wealth
    of the Indies"*:
    EDWARD L. TRUDEAU   90

6. *Among the Humblest of Created Things*:
    JEAN HENRI FABRE   94

7. *The Light That Has Not Failed*:
    CLARENCE HAWKES   97

8. *His Reward Was Hostility*:
    SUN YAT SEN   101

IV

THEY WON TRIUMPHANT FAITH

1. *Voluntary Poverty*:
    MURIEL LESTER   105

2. *A Gambler for God*:
    TOYOHIKO KAGAWA   109

3. *Up the Mountain Path*:
    SADHU SUNDAR SINGH   112

4. *"Prove Your Worth"*:
    JAMES A. K. AGGREY   115

xi

5. *The Blindfolded Player:*
   TAKEO IWAHASHI   120

6. *"Friends, Do Not Be Afraid of Life!":*
   FEODOR MIKHAYLOVICH DOSTOEVSKY   123

7. *"The Rose Above the Mould":*
   SIR WILLIAM OSLER   126

SOURCES OF QUOTATIONS   133

THEY DARED TO LIVE

I
THEY LIVED DANGEROUSLY

1. For Humanity:

HIDEYO NOGUCHI

THE PEASANT mother ran frantically from the rice field to the hut where her baby son was screaming. He had thrust his left hand into the Japanese stove and burned off his fingers. For twenty-one days and twenty-one nights she watched by his bedside.

Young Noguchi grew up to hate his crippled hand. His father was a drunkard, and the son had to work hard to pay the family's debts. Before going to school in the morning he caught fish to sell. After school he carried baggage, sometimes as much as ten miles a day. At night he tended the fires in a bath house, receiving no pay except the privilege of reading his book by the light of the stoves. There was no lamp at home, not even a stove to read by.

One day a Japanese doctor who had been trained in western science saw Hideyo's crippled hand. He began to treat it, to separate the stubs of fingers, and to release the scarred muscles that made his arm stiff and unnatural. The boy was fascinated as he watched the skilful doctor work on his hand, and he exclaimed, "I am going to be a doctor!"

He went to the city and found work as a druggist's apprentice. While reading a foreign book he discovered that Napoleon had slept only three hours a night in order to carry on his program. The ambitious lad determined to sleep less and devote all his energy to science.

One day a physician showed him a germ cell under the microscope, and Noguchi made his second decision: he would be a bacteriologist.

Without a penny he made his way to Tokyo, planning to earn his food as a rickshaw boy. He found a job that gave him a room and two yen a month, and by studying fourteen hours a day he passed his medical examination. To study abroad was his ambition.

Friends helped him to buy a ticket for America, and he arrived at the University of Pennsylvania with no money. A laboratory job was offered him, the study of snake venoms. Passionate devotion to science submerged him in work. "I have no leisure morning or night, and all night I break my bones writing the record of the day," he wrote a Japanese friend.

Eleven months after his arrival in America this twenty-four-year-old foreigner, who spoke in strange and faltering English, gave a learned address on venoms before the National Academy of Science. When hard work led him to his first achievement he observed, "Man cannot stand up in the world by ability alone. It is necessary to have virtue to correspond."

During his first year in the United States Noguchi received twenty-five dollars a month for his research work, the second year thirty-five, the third year fifty. The fourth year he won a fellowship of two thousand dollars a year, which permitted him to go to Europe to carry on special studies there.

On his return to America he lost himself in bacteriological laboratories, where he struggled to find a way to conquer syphilis, infantile paralysis, rabies, and trachoma. His fellow-workers called him "the twenty-four-hour man." He slept only a few hours at night, usually dozing in a chair with a book in his hand, waking after a brief rest to return to his work. The tireless scientist discovered secret after secret, which he released for the good of mankind, without seeking any patent or any financial return for himself.

His progress in the conquest of disease soon made his name famous, and he was honored in many countries of Europe. His heart weakened under the severe strain of work, and he was forced to take a vacation. After an absence of fifteen years he went back to Japan, to be acclaimed as one of the great scientists of his country. He stood again with his mother among the ancient temple trees where she had prayed years before for the recovery of her crippled boy.

With new enthusiasm, Dr. Noguchi came back to his American laboratory to take up the fight against yellow fever. He traveled over the world to face the unconquered plague wherever it began its reign of death. Long journeys took him to Ecuador, Mexico, Peru, and Brazil. At the same time he carried on a battle against trachoma, Oroya fever, and Rocky Mountain fever.

One of his colleagues, Doctor Stokes, had been sent to Africa to observe yellow fever and died there, a victim of the germ he was studying. Noguchi volunteered to go out and carry on the work. His friends protested, reminding him that he was fifty-one, that his heart was bad, and that he had diabetes. He laughed at the danger. "I sent Doctor Stokes and he died. I must go. I will win down there or give my life!"

The valiant doctor died a few weeks after his arrival in Africa. He caught the yellow fever while he was trying to master it; but only after he had discovered some of its deadly secrets. As his body came back across the sea there were no

3

front-page news accounts of the death of another heroic scientist. But his fellow doctors knew, and history will in time accord Dr. Hideyo Noguchi a place among the benefactors of humanity.

---

2. *The Long, Hard Trail:*
FRIDTJOF NANSEN

THE TALL, straight young Norwegian, with fair skin and bright blue eyes, went to visit the lepers with his friend, Reverend Vilhelm Holdt. This remarkable missionary was so kind to the outcast leper colony in Bergen that they called him "father." Young Fridtjof Nansen lived several years with the "father of the lepers." Father Holdt's compassion for these suffering social outcasts exerted a profound effect on the student, who determined that he also would give his life to help humanity.

Nansen loved science, the outdoors, and his fellow men. He was a brilliant student of biology. He spent his spare time sailing, skiing, tramping in the woods and mountains, always dressed in sporting clothes, moving with the swinging step of a mountain climber.

For a time he acted as a school teacher, then went abroad for advanced study, and at length was drawn into biological exploration. He longed to serve his country and the world of science. At the age of twenty-seven he crossed Greenland from coast to coast in a daring expedition and proved that there was no ice-free interior.

In 1893 he sailed on the "Fram" for a three-year expedition to the polar seas, to return as the hero of his nation. He had left the ship, which was to circle the polar sea, and with

4

one companion tried to reach the North Pole. They made the northernmost point achieved up to that time. Their homeward journey across the arctic wastes forms a saga of unparalleled achievement. They lived in a snow hut through the arctic night, without a piece of furniture or a book, without bath water or soap, or any food from civilization. Volumes of scientific observations were written by Nansen recording his adventures in the arctic region and his investigations of natural science, ocean life, and climate.

He wrote in his explorer's diary: "It is the struggle toward a goal that makes man happy. It is the game we call life that makes it worth living. It is the capacity for joy and sorrow, work, thirst, rest, toil, love, wild life, art. This glorious world is mine. I want to live, to give it of my best powers, which I feel are still lying unused, waiting for an opportunity. I see further ahead a new world to be built, and I want to build it!"

Dr. Nansen became a professor of zoology and a popular lecturer. He served as Norway's first minister to England and as a political leader of his country. Deeply affected by the World War, he cried, "What a nightmare of insanity; and no one can stop it—no one! . . . The people of Europe, 'the torch-bearers of civilization,' are devouring one another, trampling civilization underfoot, laying Europe in ruins; and who will be the gainer? And for what are they fighting? Power—only power! . . . How could it be otherwise? A civilization that sets up power as its aim and ideal cannot possibly achieve progress for humanity. It must inevitably lead hither—towards destruction."

The citizen of a non-combatant nation, the eminent scientist bent his efforts in a plea for peace and for a new international program: "There must be a regeneration—a new era with new ideals—when spiritual values will again be the end and material values only a means, when the world will

5

no longer be ruled by mediocrity and the mob. In that day, the noble spirits will lead humanity upward to the heights; every spiritual discovery, every conquest in the world of spirit will be greeted with the enthusiasm now accorded to material progress; and mankind will live a greater, simpler, more beautiful life!"

He took the lead in world reconstruction after the Great War, serving ten years as High Commissioner of the League of Nations, first for the repatriation of prisoners, later for the protection and assistance of refugees. He supervised the release and restoration of half a million prisoners who were scattered over Europe. When most nations were hostile to Soviet Russia he organized a relief expedition and went into Russia to fight plague and feed the starving. He planned the moving of a million and a half Greek fugitives who had been driven out of Asia, and got them settled in Greece. He saved thousands of Armenian refugees. While men were in despair over the world's chaos, Nansen led them courageously along the ascending trail of reconstruction.

At Geneva he toiled to break down the animosities that cursed Europe and to make the League of Nations a success. His stupendous projects for relief of the sufferers in Russia, Greece, Asia Minor, Armenia, and the Caucasus, proved the indispensable value of world co-operation. He traveled to almost every country in Europe, to the Near East, and to America, toiling to alleviate the curse of the war. When the Nobel Peace Prize was given him in 1922 he pleaded for nations to work together in honest good will to settle the world's difficulties. He used the 122,000 kroner that were awarded with the Nobel Prize to establish two agricultural stations in Russia and to help refugees in Greece.

Shortly before his death the great humanitarian spoke to

6

a group of students in Scotland: "We all have a land of Beyond to seek in life. Our part is to find the trail that leads to it. A long trail, a hard trail, maybe; but the call comes to us and we have to go. Rooted deep in the nature of every one of us is the spirit of adventure, vibrating under all our actions, making life deeper, higher and nobler. There's a whisper of the night-wind, there's a star agleam to guide us, and the Wild is calling, calling. Let us go!"

---

3. *When Dreams Come True:*

MARTHA BERRY

SITTING before the fireplace one stormy February night, Martha Berry heard a knock at the door. She opened it and faced a small and dirty boy who led a muddy pig tied to a rope. The lad looked at her anxiously.

"Please, ma'am, I'm Willie Jackson and this is my own pig. We-uns is come to school. I done carried the pig heah for my tuition. He's powuhful lean now, but he'll pick up tol'able quick."

Pig and Willie were decidedly lean, but both were welcome additions to the log-cabin school for mountain boys, which has grown into the most remarkable campus in America.

Thirty-five years ago Martha Berry got a handful of boys together to start the Berry Schools. The daughter of a wealthy and aristocratic Georgia family, Martha had ridden many times with her father into the hills. With her first glimpses into the hardship of these mountain people she felt a tormenting desire to help them. When her father died

7

and she inherited the old plantation, her mind was made up. She opened a school in the little log cabin that her father had built for her as a child, where she studied with her tutor.

Her sisters and friends tried to discourage her, arguing that she was throwing her life away and taking up a career unworthy of a southern lady. Even her old Negro mammy had said on the day her last sister went down the steps of Berry Hill a bride, "What fo' yo' gwine to do nohow, honey? Yo's wastin' yo' life sho' nuff on dem boys ovah dere. Why ain't yo' busyin' yo'se'f gettin' a home?"

Martha shook her head, "No, auntie, I have said goodbye forever to a home of my own. I have just married an *idea*. I'll have to be faithful to it, lonely as it is."

That idea is now a series of schools with a thirty-thousand-acre campus, one hundred splendid buildings, and twelve hundred students.

One glorious spring morning Martha Berry led me from her charming southern home to the school campus. As we crossed the roadway she said, "This is the gate of opportunity. Some twelve thousand students have come through it to prepare themselves for life. Any boy or any girl in the southern states who is poor and has a good character is welcome here!"

We surveyed the Women's College built by Henry Ford, the Men's College, the Foundation School, shops, water reservoir, forest, orchard, farms. The walls of a huge dairy barn had been built, but there was no roof on it. She explained, "If we find we need a new building, I get the plans and start to build it. I go as far as our money will take us and then stop. I leave it unfinished until some benefactor comes along and gives us funds to complete it. . . . It is a big responsibility to carry on the program with more

8

students coming every year and more money needed to take care of them. But I believe in having big plans. I furnish the enthusiasm and depend on my friends to carry my plans through.

"No one of my dreams has failed yet. People respond when you challenge them with a concrete appeal to help young folks. They say I have too much enthusiasm for a woman of my age. Well, I hope I never lose it!"

Above the busy school buildings, the farms, orchards, and forests, on the top of Lavendar Mountain, is a log cottage called the "House of Dreams." Here Miss Berry comes to study her enterprise and looks down upon valley vistas with new perspective. So many of her dreams have come true that the "House of Dreams" is like the abode of good fairies who wave their magic wands over this enthusiastic leader and her family of southern youth.

"Somebody once asked me what I should do when I had to stop working and got to heaven," she laughingly told me. "I said, 'Why, I am going right to St. Peter and ask him for all the cast-off crowns and stars of gold and silver. I'll melt them and send them to my schools!'"

There is an amazing student body in the Berry Schools of earnest Anglo-Saxon youth busy at work in field and laboratory, the boys in overalls, blue shirts, sleeves rolled up, the girls in uniforms of pastel shades with sun bonnets hanging down their backs like gay academic hoods. Work and beauty are the two fundamentals of their education. On a May evening I watched them march in two unwavering lines out of the Georgian chapel onto a darkening campus. Fireflies flickered about the oaks and cedars and over the sweet grass. The evening stars intermingled their light until sky and earth were joined. In their wistful faces was the determination to carry the ideals of this amazing builder of life back into a thousand hamlets scattered through the plains and hills of the southlands.

---

4. For Human Liberty:

ALBERT EINSTEIN

WHEN the electrical engineer, Hermann Einstein, tried to explain to his four-year-old son, Albert, how a compass worked, he little dreamed that his boy was destined to receive the Nobel Prize in physics and to become a world-famous scientist. The quiet and studious lad spent his boyhood in Germany and Italy, showing marked talent in mathematics, physics, and music. The father lost his money through financial reverses, and Albert went through the University of Zurich on eighty francs a month. After graduation he became a professor at Zurich, Prague, and Berlin, where his studies in physics brought him world-wide recognition. He was invited to lecture in intellectual centers of Europe, Great Britain, the Orient, and South and North America. In 1921 he received the Nobel Prize for distinguished discoveries in physics. As director of the Kaiser Wilhelm Institute for Physics, Dr. Einstein was acclaimed as one of Germany's greatest scientists.

When Adolph Hitler came into power in Germany and initiated his persecution of the Jews, Dr. Einstein condemned the nationalistic policies of the Nazi regime. In a public statement he said, "I will stay only in a country where political liberty, toleration, and equality of all citizens before the law are the rule." He was dismissed from the Prussian Academy of Science and condemned by the government. He gave up his honors in Germany, and in 1933 left for the

United States. Some time after his arrival in America I was in his home in Princeton. When I asked him if it had not been too big a sacrifice to give up his citizenship and his property for liberal ideals, he answered in his humble way, "I have made no sacrifice! I have done nothing but what a thinking man would do. It is not a matter of intellectual complexity. On issues like this a man must take a stand. I claim no credit. I could have taken no other course!"

Dr. Einstein is a sturdy, impressive figure with his shaggy head of white hair. His clothes indicated originality—a stiff shirt and wing collar, but no tie, rough tan moccasins, striped trousers such as are worn with a frock coat, and a buttoned leather jacket. His brown eyes were kindly, his quiet voice sympathetic, and his hearty laugh would disarm any listener, even those who would have kept this "dangerous pacifist" from American shores.

"Intellectual resistance to war is not enough to face present circumstances. Pacifism defeats itself under certain conditions, as in Germany today. Anyone who resists the military program will be done away with quickly and his influence brought to an end," he explained.

"We must educate, must work with the people to create a public sentiment that will outlaw war. I believe there are two features in this program of action: first, create the idea of super-sovereignty. National loyalty is limited; men must be taught to think in world terms. Every country will have to surrender a portion of its sovereignty through international co-operation. To avoid destruction, aggression must be sacrificed. Our need now is an international tribunal with authority. The League and the World Court lack the power to enforce their decisions. Though they may suffer unpopularity now, the trend of progress is toward world organization, and institutions of this type are inevitable.

11

"Second, we must face the economic causes of war. Fundamentally, our difficulty is the selfish desire of people who put profit before humanity. Individuals refuse to adopt liberal ideas; they remain provincial and self-satisfied, content with their money returns. We suffer from the ills of economic nationalism and war because these people will not control their passion for money gain. Perhaps Romain Rolland may not be far wrong in turning to social revolution as the only means of breaking the war system."

Dr. Einstein spoke with fervor. This fifty-eight-year-old Swiss Jew is more than a scholar who has spent his life in the physics laboratories of Zurich and Berlin, more than a gentle lover of the violin and nature; he is a reformer who hates war with the fervor of an Old Testament prophet.

"Of course," he went on, "I do not try to reduce life to economic forces as some do. There is a persistent emotional element in all human relations that we must cope with. As national groups we feel ourselves different from our fellow men, and we so often permit our conduct to be controlled by prejudice. We need to be educated until we understand our emotional conflicts and learn to correct them."

"Do you believe that we can change human nature?" I asked.

"We can guide human nature into new habits. That has been done throughout history. Enlightenment and discipline do lead us into better ways."

"Will we ever be able to abolish war?" I persisted.

"Yes," he answered, "I believe we can. I feel sure that we will. We must educate to do it. Our hope is in youth— who can be given emancipated views of life."

"Is religion a necessary factor in this program of education?"

"Religion can be made the basis of character instruction for youth. It should be the means with which to create more intelligent attitudes. You ask me if I believe in a purpose back of life? Every scientist wonders at the mystery of existence, and senses a creative force in the law and beauty of the universe; but I cannot define that force as an anthropomorphic God, such as many religious people believe in. Everyone has been given an endowment," he went on, "which he must strive to develop in the service of mankind. This cannot be brought to completion through the threat of a God who will punish man for sin, but only by challenging the best in human nature. To bring beauty and brotherhood into life is the chief end of man and the highest happiness."

We walked out into the blossoming garden. He drew a deep breath of the fragrant air and exclaimed, "Ah, nature!" The contagious smile was still on his face. "I am very happy with my new home in friendly America and in the liberal atmosphere of Princeton," he commented.

As I thanked him for the privilege of the interview, I said, "I hope that I may hear you lecture some time."

He laughed. "Lecture? I don't know enough to go around giving lectures or to write books. I sit some days in my study for three hours with a sheet of paper before me and during that time write down just a few little figures of some sort. No, I will never know enough to lecture or write books!"

I said goodbye, leaving the father of relativity standing in humility before his "fourth-dimension" universe.

---

5. *Redeemer of the Underworld:*
THOMAS MOTT OSBORNE

ONE DAY in 1913, a prisoner, number 33,333x, walked through the gates of Auburn Prison. He was booked as

"Tom Brown," but his real name was Thomas Mott Osborne. Through his own choice he was entering this penitentiary to learn how convicts were treated and how he might help the criminals of America. No one of the 1,400 men in gray knew who this newcomer was. He became a part of the institutional routine, and soon sensed the fear and deceit that characterized prison life.

He discovered that "in prison, as elsewhere, when men are dominated by fear, brutality is the inevitable result." H was sent to the "cooler," a black iron cage, full of stale air and vermin. He had to sleep on the floor, for the cage was bare of all furniture. Three gills of water were the supply for twenty-four hours. The dark, the silence, and the choking air terrified him. In the next cage was a sick man. Near by was the death chamber. The troubled words of his companions and the horror of the cage almost drove him mad before he was released from punishment.

As he went from his torture back to the prison he prayed, "May I be an instrument in Thy hands, God, to help others see the light. And may no impatience, prejudice, or pride of opinion on my part, hinder the service Thou hast given me to do."

Osborne had been born under the shadow of Auburn prison. As a boy he played near its towering walls. The specter of this impressive landmark haunted him as a child. He had been taken on a visit within the gray gates, and the memory of it tracked him through life: "The dark, scowling faces bent over their tasks; the hideous striped clothing, which carried with it an unexplainable sense of shame; the ugly, close-cropped heads and unshaven faces; the horrible sinuous lines of outcast humanity crawling along in the dreadful lockstep; the whole thing aroused such terror in my imagination that I never recovered from the painful impression. All the nightmares and evil dreams of my

14

childhood centered about the figure of the escaped convict."

Wealthy, well educated, a leader in state politics and civic affairs, Osborne was ideally equipped for his career. W. R. George, of the George Junior Republic, had proved what could be done with undisciplined boys when the proper environment was created, and won the loyal support of the prominent Auburn citizen. Mr. Osborne thought of George's suggestion that the program he had worked out among boys might be applied to prison life. In 1904 he began to develop principles of prison reform, but was not given an opportunity to try out his ideas until 1913, when he was appointed chairman of a prison commission in the state of New York.

The prisons of this epoch were characterized by small cells, absolute silence, iron chains, cages, handcuffs, whippings, dungeons, and the strait jacket. Many prisoners who survived sentence went out victims of insanity or tuberculosis. In one penitentiary men were placed in dungeons twenty feet below the ground, made to bend over double, their heads two feet from the ground, arms and legs manacled, forced to stand bent for hours. Osborne knew the facts, and challenged the assumption that men in prison were all perverse and vicious. He believed they would respond if they were treated as other men, and that their habits might in many cases be reconstructed by humane, enlightened methods.

After serving his voluntary sentence as "Tom Brown," he began to set forth these new precepts for prison life, and to test them out through the co-operation of the Auburn prison staff. Prisoners came to him with their troubles. He became a sort of Messiah; they spoke of him as the "redeemer of the underworld." Later he became warden and organized the Mutual Welfare League. Under self-government, guards were dispensed with at meals, discipline was self-administered, public gatherings were held. In 1914 the 1,400 inmates gathered for the first Sunday service ever held during the one hundred and four years of the prison's history. Sunday, which had been called the "devil's day," became a day of useful activity. Entertainments were organized and given by the prisoners. Men were let out into the sun and onto the grass, which many of them had not seen for months. The new warden's plan was "We will turn this prison from a scrap heap into a repair shop."

When he became warden at Sing Sing prison he brought the 1,496 men together in the dining hall, "white faces in a sea of gray," and talked to them in a new language. "Unless I can do you some good there is no earthly reason for me to come here." Sing Sing was transformed as Auburn had been. But his humane and progressive policies met terrific opposition. Some said the penitentiary had become a "joy palace"; that prisoners were being "coddled." Politicians wanted to keep the prisons a part of their spoils system. Warden Osborne was not interested in grafting off human spoils. Foes fought against him in Auburn, Sing Sing, and Portsmouth, where he put his theories into operation.

Political enemies drove him out of Sing Sing. He was indicted for perjury, for neglect of duty, for failure to exercise general supervision over the government and discipline, and because he did not "deport himself in a manner as to command the respect, esteem, and confidence of the inmates." This indictment brought a storm of protest, and helped to make public the political exploitation of American prisons.

Mr. Osborne retired from Portsmouth prison in 1920. In 1921 he wrote to a friend, "It is no use talking, the politicians are too strong for us." He studied the prisons of the country, became a special investigator on penal problems, and a world-recognized figure. He wrote in 1924: "If I seem impatient or intolerant, be kind enough to consider what must be the state of mind of a man after my experience; I have shared in the joys of discovery of a system which solves a great problem; I have been privileged to work it into practical shape; I have proved it at the head of two institutions—finding in myself unexpected power to lead prisoners into a right way of acting and thinking. Then I have seen this work so patiently built up, destroyed; sometimes brutally in a day, sometimes by long but steady undermining, until there is now but little left. And I am condemned to heart-breaking idleness; realizing what I can do to benefit mankind, and not permitted to do it."

Two years later he fell dead in the streets of Auburn. At the funeral service in his local church, thoughtful people began to pay tribute to a pioneer who had been broken by reactionary prison leaders, the yellow press, and political machines. And after that "Tom Brown's" body returned to Auburn prison, and 1,400 men passed in front of his open casket.

Two endless lines of dingy, gray-clad men
Come up the stairway, parting to pass him there,
Tom Brown, Commander, wearing the Navy's blue,
Wearing its gold, Osborne, the Legionnaire.

Silent, they shuffle past, tight at the throat,
Dim in the eyes, with shoulders that lift and shake—
Eyes that have looked on shameful things, hands that have
    slain,
Feet that have fled away from stern pursuit,
Arms that have crushed out virtue, lips that have lied,
Throats that have blasphemed, claws that have curved for
    loot,
Endlessly they go by, their faces gray
Into the chapel bare, to think—and pray.*

* From a poem by Adelaide B. Mead.

17

In the winter of 1936, ten years after the death of Thomas Mott Osborne, a massive bronze statue was dedicated in his memory in the home town of Auburn. Twenty tons of Maine granite form the base for his commanding figure, which stands in front of the city high school. Notable Americans assembled; eulogies were made in praise of the pioneer. Newspapers resurrected his name and began to praise him as a great American.

Even a short decade can make a difference in a nation's estimate of its citizens!

---

6. "Truth Is the Country of the Free Man":

ROMAIN ROLLAND

THE YOUNG professor of music was obsessed by one idea—through music he could bring the nations of the world together. Music spoke above nationalities in a voice that taught men the ways of peace. Although he was a teacher at the Sorbonne, the gay crowds of Paris turned a deaf ear to his cause. Therefore he determined to write plays which would present on the stage the universal cry of man for peace. But the Parisians chose vaudeville in preference. Undaunted, he tackled biography. He discovered that all great men were internationalists; and he wrote the stories of Beethoven, Michelangelo, Tolstoy, and Gandhi. But no one of these men lived amid the nationalistic, war-minded twentieth-century Europe. He had to create a new man for a new age. This creation led to the novel, *Jean Christophe,* which pleaded for an intermingling of cultures in Europe and a warless world.

Two years after its publication, the World War began.

The valiant writer, M. Romain Rolland, did everything he could to keep France and Germany from fighting. He tried to organize a Tribunal of the Spirit, summoning the intellectuals of Europe to confer and perfect a plan to stop the war. No one would join him in Switzerland. He remained there throughout the war, where he tried to pierce through the hatreds and fears that suffocated Europe, and to hold up the facts from both sides of the conflict. He carried on a friendly relief center, searching for lost soldiers, writing letters of sympathy to parents whose sons had been sacrificed, corresponding with young people in many nations, urging them on in their revolt against war and in their quest for peace.

His novel, *Clerambault,* is the record of a Paris professor and his protest against the conflict. Professor Clerambault sends out his manifestoes to the people of the world until he is assassinated by the war leaders of Europe. He cries, "What have I to do with your nations? Can you expect me to love or hate a nation? It is men that I love or hate, and in all nations you will find the noble, the base, and the ordinary man. I have brothers in every nation, enemy or ally, and those you would thrust upon me as compatriots are not always the nearest. The families of our souls are scattered through the world. Let us reunite them! You are mad, peoples of the earth; instead of defending your country, you are killing her. You are your country and the enemies are your brothers. Millions of God's creatures, love one another."

Since those bloody days M. Rolland has remained in Switzerland, fighting with prophetic zeal against a return of war. I found him disheartened when I visited him at Villeneuve. He was then in his sixty-fifth year. . . . His tall figure was bent with the long conflict. Hair and mustache were snow white. But the fire of an undaunted hope burned in his blue eyes. He welcomed me warmly and we talked until late into the night.

"It is terrifyingly difficult for the idealist today. Prophets of peace are still despised while war lords are acclaimed. Those who suffer for the freedom of new ways are alone! Independent spirits seem to be spending themselves in puerile struggle against the entrenched error of old ways. Progress toward understanding is almost negligible.

"I am looking to the Orient now," he went on. "We are bent on destroying western civilization. Wiser men of the East may guide us. There is Gandhi, who may be the master statesman of the highest social motive. Most westerners are not fit to sit in judgment on Gandhi, limited patriots that they are! The Eternal Spirit has spoken in many ways and to many souls scattered through the ages of time—to the East as well as to the West. Wisdom from the Orient may teach us to practise harmony and compromise."

He came back again and again to his favorite theme, the reconciling of the nations. "We human beings belong to no one nation, but to the whole of humanity. When I published *Jean Christophe*, my first letter was from a young Chinese who wrote, 'I am Jean Christophe. You have laid bare the struggle of my life.' Then came other messages with the same confession from seekers in all parts of the globe. Every one of us can grow beyond his nation and become a citizen of the world."

He spoke of the impulse to share life with other nations and races, and the passion to know the universal truth which had propelled him since youth. "My career has been possessed by certain inexplicable ideals. I grew up in a humble home in Burgundy under the devoted care of my parents, but something more than environment and training influenced me."

Since that night the pilgrim has traveled in an unexpected direction in his quest for peace. The annal of this pilgrimage is his five-volume novel, *The Soul Enchanted*. His impassioned seekers revolt against the baseness of the World

War as it poisons Paris and suffocates Europe with its hatred. His youthful hero, Marc, looked out upon the world of November 11, 1918: "Everything had been destroyed and the wind that blew over the field of ruin was laden with the stench of the charnel house. Where could youth rebuild the world? They knew nothing; they could see nothing in the smoking chaos. Everything was lacking except guns!"

Marc tried pacifism, non-resistance, fascism, but was driven at length in desperation to communism. His sweetheart, Assia, represents the new Russia. The frustration and futility of life drew Marc to Assia and her Soviet crusade. "The current of the stream bears us along. We have but to hold the tiller of the boat. The will of the stream be done!"

Rolland shrinks from the violence of revolution, but the impotence of peace crusades and the impending ruin of war compel him. He deserts Gandhi and chooses Lenin's way, believing that the Russian program will bring a new world order.

"Wars—war; of all business the most enormous and the most juicy, juicy with gold, juicy with blood, for the magnates, manufacturers, and traffickers of the metallurgic and chemical industries, for the monopolies and trusts of wheat and of cotton and of accumulated stocks of merchandise; and it is juicy with dividends and coupons for the bourgeoisie and their shares. Real peace demands that the masters of war be eliminated. They will be so only after the assault upon their Bastilles. Those of Russia have already fallen. When will it be the turn of ours? Are we ready?"

By nature a man of peace, an artist who loves music and beauty, a historian who knows the curse of violence, M. Rolland struggles to justify this departure from his ideals: "Only those are wretched whose energy is not equal to their faith; those who have nothing to sacrifice themselves for. It is a hard epoch, it is cruel, but it is beautiful to be strong.

One must be of the stature of one's time. . . . The free spirits (idealists of peace) had forgotten the primary essentials of successful agriculture. To make the wheat grow, the ground must first be cleared, freed from stones, the thickets burned, and after that one must press heavily on the plowshare and drive the furrow straight and long and deep. The 'august gesture of the sower' is not enough. We must use force, we must force the resisting earth, force the oxen straining under the yoke, force our muscles, force our hearts!"

Some of his admirers argue that Rolland, the free spirit, will not long remain a disciple of Lenin. But he is an old man and his young wife is a Russian. He may now be near the end of his quest, and will have to say to his contemporaries, "Non moi, mon frère, mais voi!"

---

7. *"Playing a Good Part
in a Great Scheme":*

EDWARD A. WILSON

AT THE age of nine he announced to his father that he was going to be a naturalist. He promptly invested a sovereign in skinning and stuffing tools and took his first lesson in taxidermy. While his classmates were busy at games, young Edward Wilson took to the fields and woods. He would be out with the dawn, carrying a piece of bread in his pocket, tramping the country, making notes on cloud formations, flower buds, and bird songs. One of his sisters tells of his return home one morning with two plover's eggs in his pocket. On studying the eggs he found that they were about ready to hatch. Without waiting for his breakfast he set out to carry them back three miles to their nest. His father, a doctor of medicine, had been trained to shift for himself in the out-doors. He taught his son to travel on foot long distances with only a few shillings for spending money.

Edward disciplined his body by sleeping on the ground under the open sky, and trained his senses to perceive the movements, colors, and sounds of nature. He kept up his outdoor ramblings during his college days at Cambridge. He fished the Cam at three in the morning, and took a present of choice trout to the master, who was so conscientious that he "sent him down" for breaking rules. But the young fisherman had hooked the finest trout of the season; and the master ate them.

The tall, thin, individualistic student rowed in his college boat and won the university prize for diving, although he failed in his medical examinations. He found a class of Sunday-school boys and made the "little beasts" behave by reading to them from Fowler's *Tales from the Birds*.

At medical school in London he became active in the Caius Mission in the slums. He took charge of the children's service on Sunday mornings; in the afternoon he instructed a class of a dozen boys. Two nights in the week he gave entertainments for the mission folks. Work in the Battersea slums was added to his schedule of medical study and hospital duty, and to his sketching and wide reading. He illustrated for Charles Walker a book on fishing flies. During these two years he made a careful reading of the New Testament, writing his own commentary. These annotations indicate a profound grasp on religion. "Every bit of truth that comes into a man's heart burns in him and forces its way out, either in his actions or in his words," he said. "Truth is like a lighted lamp in that it cannot be hidden away in the darkness because it carries its own light."

"In Wilson's presence," a friend explained, "everything mean or base seemed to shrivel up." Excessive work made him thin and pale. He walked to the hospital. Arriving at ten in the morning, he worked all day, lunching on biscuits and milk. He walked back to Battersea for dinner, and until eight o'clock he was "talking, praying, and singing in a positive reek of Battersea children." He read in bed until two or three in the morning. Worried over his temperature and dizziness, he went to the doctor. The diagnosis was a blow—pulmonary tuberculosis. He had to leave at once for Davos, in Switzerland.

The Swiss village was a lonely place piled high with snow. He was so weak that he could not even ride on a toboggan. There was "nothing but idle loafing, terribly depressing and demoralizing. My most violent exercise is a ten minutes' walk. The only thing I miss is a perambulator." During this quest for health his mystical nature developed. He turned more to religion. His amazing philosophy is expressed in these words to his future wife, which he wrote at that time:

"Look at life carelessly. The only things worth being disappointed in or worrying about are in ourselves, not in externals. Take life as it comes and do what lies straight in front of you. It's only real carelessness about one's own will, and absolute hope and confidence in God's, that can teach one to believe that whatever is, is best. Don't you think this is the key to happiness in an apparently spoilt and disappointing life?"

His ascetic ideal was St. Francis of Assisi. God, nature, and humanity were mingled in his religion. He learned to find his inspiration in the things close at hand. "A happy life is not built up of tours abroad and pleasant holidays, but of little clumps of violets noticed by the roadside, almost hidden away so that only those can see them who have God's peace and love in their hearts; in one long continuous chain of little joys; little whispers from the spiritual world; little gleams of sunshine on our daily work. . . . So long as I have stuck to Nature and the New Testament I have only got happier and happier every day."

The frail philosopher won his way back to health. Although he did not yet achieve his old-time rugged strength, he was able to complete his medical course and marry his devoted fiancée, Miss Souper. A few words in his mother's diary describe him at this time, "a body so frail and delicate, a noble soul and spiritual."

Captain Scott was setting out aboard his ship, the Discovery, for a scientific expedition to the Antarctic in 1901. He wanted the young naturalist and doctor to join his party. Edward Wilson was well equipped except for his health. He accepted; and as soon as the voyage was under way he began to regain his old-time vigor. He became, in Captain Scott's words, "the life and soul of the party, the organizer of all amusements, the always good-tempered and cheerful one, the ingenious person who could get round all difficulties." Self-discipline had given him a poise that made him the most beloved man on the ship. "He was the kind of man one would give one's life for willingly."

Wilson made a valuable collection of sketches on Antarctic geography and animal life. He sketched with frost-bitten fingers and snow-blinded eyes to complete his famous drawings. "My eyes have been in a sorry state all day from sketching with sun-glare, streaming with water and very painful. Sketching in the Antarctic is not all joy, for apart from the fact that your fingers are all thumbs and you don't know the fact or where they are till they warm up again, you can sketch only when your eyes stop running, one eye at a time, through a narrow slit in snow-goggles." He made pencil drawings with notes on color, and did his coloring on the ship at night by the light of candles crudely fashioned from tallow and blubber.

The Discovery arrived in England in September, 1904. Dr. Wilson was caught in a whirlwind of activity—social functions, addresses, books to write, books to illustrate. He was an authority on antarctic zoology. His most popular lecture in Queen's Hall was delivered when he was suffering with rheumatism and in need of money; but he gave the returns to the Caius College Mission in the London slums.

From 1905 to 1910 he engaged in the study of the grouse disease that was destroying the birds of England. He visited the moors of England and Scotland, sleeping outdoors to learn the habits of the grouse or to catch a drop of dew for microscopic examination. He dissected more than two thousand birds. His suitcase containing the studies of two years was stolen in Glasgow, and he had to do his experiments all over again. He illustrated numerous books, and completed a wide collection of bird and animal studies.

The ardent worker wrote at this time, "I get such a feeling of the absolute necessity to be at something always, and at every hour, day and night, before the end may come or I have done a decent portion of what I was expected to do; each minute is of value. . . . I feel that every picture I draw will live and affect something after our death."

Scott's second expedition to the Antarctic began in 1910. Edward Wilson could not resist the invitation to go. He was in the small party that reached the Pole late in December, 1911. On their return march they were caught in a blizzard at a point eleven miles from One-Ton Depot, where there were provisions that would have kept them alive for weeks. His last words were written to his wife, as he lay with Captain Scott and another companion in a tent covered with snow, freezing to death:

"Don't be unhappy—all is for the best. We are playing a good part in a great scheme arranged by God himself, and

all is well. . . . All the things I had hoped to do with you
after this Expedition are as nothing now, but there are
greater things for us to do in the world to come."

---

8. Fraternity:

EUGENE VICTOR DEBS

Susan B. Anthony was coming to town! The "female
firebrand" from the East was to speak in Terre Haute. Even
the Occidental Literary Club, which had brought Wendell
Phillips to the city, was afraid to sponsor the suffragette.
One young member challenged, "All right, if you're afraid.
I'll handle the matter myself!"

It was more of an undertaking than Eugene Debs had an-
ticipated. He hired the hall and met her at the station. He
escorted her through the main street. Her hat was on one
side of her head; she chattered as they walked. A street
loafer guffawed loudly. Gene stopped abruptly and faced
the scoffer. There was fire in his wide blue eyes. The laughing stopped. But that evening there was no audience. The
young idealist was fortunate to get the despised radical safely
out of Terre Haute. Even his friends were disgusted with
him.

At eighteen, this blue-eyed, muscular giant was firing a
freight engine on the seventy-mile run from his home town
to Indianapolis. He had a love for the railroad and became
a pioneer in the Brotherhood of Locomotive Engineers and
Firemen. The early years of his life were given to the organization of the railroad workers of America. At thirty
he was elected a member of the Indiana legislature and mar-

ried Katherine Metzel, a golden-haired girl of German descent. This was his first love, and one that lasted through turbulent years. •

The organizer of railway brotherhoods became the leader of the Socialist party in the United States. He was a sturdy campaigner for the rights of the laboring man. He was a socialist but not a communist. When Russian revolutionists began their persecutions, Debs sent a cablegram to Lenin: "I protest with all civilized people in the name of our common humanity against the execution of any of the Social Revolutionaries or the unjust denial of their liberty. Soviet Russia can set an example by refusing to follow the practices of world-wide czardom, and should uphold the higher standards we seek to erect and profess to observe."

Debs was a revolutionist, but he thought of a bloodless revolution that was to come about through peaceful and democratic methods, not by guns and executions.

With the beginning of the World War, Eugene Debs was outspoken in his opposition to the war. It was a violation of his faith in international brotherhood. He was arrested in June, 1917, after a speech in Cleveland, and tried by a jury of farmers. He made his own defense, denying that he had attempted to cause insubordination, mutiny, disloyalty, and refusal of duty in the military forces of the United States. He denied that he had incited resistance to the United States or promoted the cause of the Imperial German Government. He reiterated his belief in the need for social reform to "bring about a change that shall do away with the rule of the great body of the people by a relatively small class and establish in this country an industrial and social democracy. . . .

"The minority are right. In every age there have been a few heroic souls who have been in advance of their time, who have been misunderstood, maligned, persecuted, sometimes put to death. Long after their martyrdom, monuments were erected to them and garlands were woven for their graves.

"I have been accused of having obstructed the war. I admit it. Gentlemen, I abhor war. I would oppose the war if I stood alone. When I think of a cold, glittering steel bayonet being plunged in the white, quivering flesh of a human being I recoil with horror. I have often wondered if I could take the life of a fellow man, even to save myself. . . .

"I do not believe that the shedding of blood bears any actual testimony to patriotism, to lead a country to civilization.

"Gentlemen, I am the smallest part of this trial. I have lived long enough to appreciate my own personal insignificance in relation to a great issue that involves the welfare of the whole people. What you may choose to do to me will be of small consequence. After all, I am not on trial here. There is an infinitely greater issue that is being tried in this court, though you may not be conscious of it. American institutions are on trial here before a court of American citizens. The future will tell."

The American people were at war. The jury of farmers deliberated for five hours and gave the verdict, "Guilty as charged in the indictment." Debs received the sentence of ten years in the penitentiary with these words, "I can see the dawn of a better day of humanity. The people are awakening. In due course of time they will come into their own."

In Atlanta penitentiary he determined to dedicate the balance of his life to prison reform. He drew up his prison creed:

> "While there is a lower class I am in it;
> While there is a criminal element I am of it;
> While there's a soul in prison I am not free."

The prisoners' problems were his problems. "There is something about Gene that wins the prisoners. He loves them. When he talks to them they are different," the chaplain explained.

He stood one day with his fellow-offenders listening to the convict band play. There was a mass of two thousand men.

"I hope God was looking that way," said Debs. "Faces furrowed deep with pain and sorrow and seamed and scarred with sin and shame! White faces, black faces, boys' faces! A young convict, a mere child, mounted the stand and sang the sweetness of his boyish soul into the hungering hearts of that sublimely great aggregation of his fellow-convicts. A solemn hush fell upon the intensely dramatic scene. It is etched upon my consciousness as vividly as if traced in living flame. Again the faces! Prison pallor touched to life again! Lips quivering and tears trembling on the sunken cheeks of sad faces! I saw and felt it all. Strange, weird, ghastly, touchingly beautiful, and infinitely appealing and pathetic! My heart stilled its breathing, and deep within me a convict bowed and wept."

During these days in Atlanta an incident occurred that gave proof of the brotherly spirit in Eugene Debs' heart, and which impresses even those who cannot share his philosophy of politics. Word went out that a Negro murderer was dying in the penitentiary hospital. He kept calling for his mother, but she could not come. The "old agitator" heard the report and got permission to go visit the Negro. Placing his hand on the man's feverish forehead he spoke to him in his most brotherly way. The Negro in his delirium murmured, "Ah, mammy, I know'd yo'd come."

Calling for a rocking chair, he picked the Negro up in his arms and rocked him, singing in his best dialect, "Swing low, sweet chariot, comin' for to carry me home." As the

Negro died, a strange silence settled over the hospital. At that moment there was no distinction between rich and poor, black or white. Fraternity had broken down the barriers.

President Harding pardoned the objector to war. The penitentiary roared a farewell salutation. Debs felt the impulse to turn back. He had no right to leave those haunting, tearful faces! But there was his cause—prison reform—and Kate was waiting for him in Terre Haute! He went out to take up a new crusade, which was to last but a few weeks. He had to lay down his banner on October 20, 1926.

---

9. *"She Stuck to Hull House*
All Her Life":

JANE ADDAMS

THESE houses aren't pretty like ours. They're ugly and small. There's nowhere to play. Why do people live here?"

Jane Addams was riding with her father through the shanty section of Freeport.

"Because they have no money to live in better places," Mr. John Addams replied.

The girl felt uncomfortable; she thought of her own spacious home in neighboring Cedarville.

"When I'm a grown-up lady, I'm going to live in a great big house, but I don't want it to be near other nice ones. I want to live right next door to poor people, and the children can play in my yard."

"That's a fine plan," he encouraged her. "I hope you *will* carry it out some day."

The child had lost her mother when she was two. Shortly afterward she fell ill with typhoid fever, which spoiled the curls in her hair. Later she contracted tuberculosis of the spine and was left with a crooked back. She was a frail girl who held her head to one side.

Finishing her course at Rockford Seminary, she departed for the Woman's Medical College in Philadelphia to prepare to become a doctor among the poor. The shock of her father's death caused her to break down and enter another nightmare of suffering with her back. A noted specialist advised that she would not live a year. She was able to reach her sister's home, where she lay in a plaster cast for months. Strapped into a steel-ribbed leather jacket, she learned to walk again. For eight years after graduation from college she spent most of her time in hospitals, with a few months of travel abroad.

She was impatient with the art galleries in the capitals of Europe; her interest was in the slums. In the East End of London she saw misery that shamed her for the luxury of her life. In Coburn she watched peasant women carry heavy casks of hot beer on their backs, with scalding drops splashing upon their heads and shoulders. She ran to protest to the brewery owner.

"Look at those women," she cried. "Couldn't the beer be carried in some other way?"

"Ach, Himmel, und who says it should pe?" he blustered, very red in the face.

"I do!" replied Jane, firmly.

The old purpose kept hammering away in her brain, "I must give my life for these neglected people!" There was a course of study at Johns Hopkins University and further ordeals of sickness. She was longing to build that house next door to the poor and have the children play in her yard.

In 1889, when she was twenty-nine years old, she founded in Chicago her famous social settlement, Hull House. She held open house for the foreign born, the Negroes, the forgotten people of America's slums. "Hull House was simply begun by two of us going down into the district to live," she explained later. "We had no definite idea as to what we were to do, but we hoped, by living among the people, to learn what was needed there and to help out." She and her friend, Ellen Starr, had very little money. They did the janitor service themselves, washing windows and scrubbing floors.

Miss Addams worked for the uplift of children, for better homes, for health and literacy. She served as garbage inspector in her ward of Chicago to do her bit for civic improvement. She said to Chicago, "Something must be done about conditions. The division of the city into rich and poor, into clean and unclean streets, is beginning to make us all uncomfortable. The rich need the poor as much as the poor need the rich."

Sewing was carried on by the garment makers in slum sweat shops. Hull House took the lead in exposing conditions and agitating for reform. A bribe of $50,000 was said to have been offered to stop Jane Addams, but she went ahead until she got a change. She helped to foster the juvenile court, clinics, playgrounds, and visiting nurses; fought child labor; pioneered in striving for insurance against unemployment, old age, and poverty. She was a crusader for woman suffrage and equal rights for women.

Her first famous book, *Twenty Years at Hull House,* was followed by a second and even more significant one, *Second Twenty Years at Hull House.* She clung to her ideals and to her program for human betterment. A stubborn resoluteness made her unswerving. Mrs. Carrie Chapman Catt said that Miss Addams headed her list of America's greatest women. "She stuck to Hull House all her life. She made it a success. She stuck through when it was a success. That is a rare thing to do—to stick to a success."

Jane Addams' first crusade was against poverty. Her other crusade was against war. She helped organize the Woman's International League for Peace and Freedom in 1915, and served as its president for fourteen years. She toured Europe in 1915 and tried to generate sufficient sentiment among the women to stop the World War. When the war ended she gave herself even more unstintedly in the crusade for peace.

With the Nobel Prize that was given for her peace work came this tribute: "In honoring Miss Addams we also pay homage to the work which women can do for the cause of peace and fraternity among nations. Her quiet personality creates an atmosphere of good will, which instinctively calls forth the best in all."

Through her seventy-five years she held resolutely to a vision. She was true to the promise she made as a girl of eight, "I'm going to build myself a house among the slum children and let them play in my yard." She kept faith with the spirit of her father, who mourned to his twelve-year-old daughter over the death of Mazzini, the Italian liberator. She took up Mazzini's mantle and helped to extend his dream of a brotherhood of the world.

---

10. "Life Is Painting a Picture,
   Not Doing a Sum":

JUSTICE OLIVER WENDELL HOLMES

Son of the famous American poet, educated in the best schools of Boston, Oliver Wendell Holmes Junior grew up under the tutelage of Ralph Waldo Emerson and Theodore Parker. Harvard College and the Civil War formed the training grounds upon which the character of the young man was shaped. At the age of twenty he entered the Union army. While serving with the Twentieth Massachusetts Volunteers, at Ball's Bluff, a cannon ball struck him in the stomach and knocked him flat. A sergeant picked him up. Within three minutes he was struck again by a conical "minie" ball, which entered his breast above the heart. A surgeon, considering him mortally wounded, ordered him to be carried across the river. He was taken to a Philadelphia hospital, where his father found him and moved him to Boston in a railway car.

In the battle of Antietam he was shot through the neck. At Chancellorsville a piece of shrapnel shattered his heel. His father rushed from the North again and carried his son, now a captain, back home to spend a long term in the hospital. The young New England aristocrat discovered the heroism of the common man as he suffered in camp and on battlefield. The lesson of the war was burned into his mind.

A bachelor of law at twenty-five, Holmes was admitted to the bar in 1867, practised in Boston, and five years later married Fanny Dixwell, with whom he spent "a fifty-six-year honeymoon." They were both high spirited and talented; and often ran to fires together in later years when they lived in Washington.

A professor of law at Harvard, he taught: "A law school does not undertake to teach success. The business of a law school is not sufficiently described when you merely say that it is to teach law, or to make lawyers. It is to teach law in the grand manner, and to make great lawyers. . . . The law is the calling of thinkers. . . .

"No man has earned the right to intellectual ambition until he has learned to lay his course by a star which he has never seen—to dig by the divining rod for springs which he may never reach. In saying this, I point to that which will

35

make your study heroic. For I say to you in all sadness of conviction, that to think great thoughts you must be heroes as well as idealists. Only when you have worked alone—when you have felt around you a black gulf of solitude more isolating than that which surrounds the dying man, and in hope and in despair have trusted to your own unshaken will—then only will you have achieved. Thus only can you gain the secret isolated joy of the thinker, who knows that, a hundred years after he is dead and forgotten, men who never heard of him will be moving to the measure of his thought."

For twenty years he served in the Supreme Judicial Court of Massachusetts and for thirty years in the Supreme Court of the United States. The Justice's legal mind was touched with a spirit of liberalism. He championed freedom of the press, speech, opinion, and assembly. He gave many progressive minority reports with his sympathetically minded co-worker, Justice Brandeis.

When he was a young man, Justice Holmes made the resolution that he would not read newspapers, and he stuck to it all his life. This was a protective measure he used to keep his mind from being carried away by the current ideas that ebbed and flowed about him. He testified that this abstinence developed clarity of judgment. During the World War he refused to read the war reports and casualty lists. One day he said he felt, while walking in the balmy air, that the war had ended. The war had choked freedom and good will in human hearts. These restraints were lifted, and he knew that humanity was again at peace.

For twenty-four years Mr. Holmes did not miss a session of the Supreme Court. He carried on his duties until he was ninety-one. He had commented at eighty, "I always thought that when I got to be four score I could wrap up my life in a scroll, tie a pink ribbon around it, put it away in a drawer, and go around doing the things I wanted to do. But

I learned that when you have taken one trench there is always a new firing line beyond." Beyond eighty he postponed retirement, saying that he would quit when his work ceased to be fun.

The last opinion he read was in January, 1932. His voice that day was clear and his reasoning luminous. As the court attendant helped him on with his coat, he said quietly, "I won't be in tomorrow." Shunning public demonstrations, he made a quiet exit from the post of service he had honored so long.

Chief Justice Charles Evans Hughes said of him, "Mr. Holmes is not old, but invincibly young. He is as lovable as ever, with the warm heart that resists the chill of years. One could search the whole world in vain for any personality more electric and inspiring in contacts. . . . The most beautiful and the rarest thing in the world is a complete human life, unmarred, unified by intelligent purpose and uninterrupted accomplishment, blessed by great talent employed in the worthiest activities, with a deserved fame never dimmed and always growing. Such a rarely beautiful life is that of Mr. Justice Holmes."

Interviewed when he was ninety, a visitor asked him if he was as optimistic as his friend Lord Bryce about the political experiment undertaken in America.

"Are you in despair?" Mr. Holmes demanded. "I'm not."

"Despair is a strong word," the visitor countered; "perhaps downcast would be better."

"I'm not downcast, either," the Justice said, "I look abroad, and see other kinds of governments functioning no better than ours, if as well. And everywhere I see an increasing tendency to refer questions of popular import to the popular will."

He held his faith unto the end in the common sense of reasonable men.

"Life is painting a picture, not doing a sum." His words

ring like an echo after him. "Man is born a predestined idealist, for he is born to act. To act is to affirm the worth of an end; to persist in affirming the worth of an end is to make an ideal. . . . The root at once of joy and beauty is to put out as compact and solid a piece of work as one can, to try to make it first rate, and to leave it unadvertised.

"I have always thought that not a place or power or popularity makes the success that one desires, but the trembling hope that one has come near to an ideal."

II

THEY BLAZED NEW TRAILS

1. A Sensitive Conscience:

JOHN GALSWORTHY

I AM MORE interested in fighting war today than any other thing," said Mr. John Galsworthy when he was visiting America a few months before he died. "Unless we can learn to avert war, there is no use in living! In 1914 we might drift on this issue, but to refuse today to fight war is to act the rôle of a fool! England and America must stand together as brothers in keeping the peace of the world!"

As Mr. Galsworthy told me of his plan to devote the balance of his life to the outlawry of war, I thought of his aristocratic background—the son of one of London's leading lawyers, educated at Harrow and Oxford, with wealth that permitted him to travel over the world and enjoy everything worth while. With world-wide popularity as a writer, he kept a conscience that did not permit him to forget others. He refused knighthood from the king, explaining that his honors in literature were already more than he deserved. The message of most of his novels and plays is barbed with satire on the smug habits of English society and kindled by the demand for reform. He was an aristocrat of aristocrats, but a very human man with a sensitive conscience.

"Has it been worth it," I asked him, "these forty years you have spent writing and struggling to make society better?" His strong face was lighted with conviction as he answered, "Indeed it has! I have seen marked changes! Since I wrote my play *Strife,* capital and labor have learned to practise better economic relationships. Humanity has demanded more humane treatment of prisoners since I published *Justice.* We still have foes to fight. The sinister forces of extreme nationalism and the war system are the enemies that now confront us. I have seen humanity overcome one set of prejudices and make life that much nobler. It is the duty of the oncoming generation to meet and master the prejudices that now enslave us to false patriotism and war!"

His broad face and semi-bald head were tanned by three months' vacation in Arizona. White hair and heavy eyebrows, a strong jaw and square upright shoulders gave him the bearing of English aristocracy. But he was delightfully humble and straightforward. The artistic hands which had penned some of the finest prose of our century were large and strong and spoke of intimate contact with the world.

Soon after his death I visited Bury House, his summer home in Sussex, England. It is a place of rare beauty. I felt at once it was a home that had been lived in by a happy couple.

The love of John and Ada Galsworthy is a romance like that of Pierre and Marie Curie, of Ramsay and Margaret MacDonald. Her confidence in his literary ability inspired him to continue writing until he won fame with *The Man of Property.* She brought the beauty to his life upon which he depended more and more as the years passed. She copied the manuscript of his books, served as a devoted secretary, and planned pilgrimages to all sections of the world in quest of inspiration.

Mrs. Galsworthy's heart was heavy with loneliness as we walked about the rooms of Bury House. She spoke of his sympathy for others. He could not shut his eyes to human need. He was always trying to help somebody or some cause. A book such as *Caravan* portrays individuals who won his sympathy—an old cab driver, a London vendor, a kindly German who was hated by his English neighbors during the World War, a poor chap who cared for stray cats, a lonely man who loved beauty. As a novelist he studied the pharisaic habits that permit men to accept distinctions in morals, clothes, and caste; and he took a rap at these hypocrisies.

His niece, Mrs. Rudolf Sauter, said to me, "He was the kindest man I ever knew, always gentle and unselfish. When he was not writing to expose some wrong, he was busy building houses for the village people, helping the town nurse, some neighbor, a vagabond, or a foreign exile."

A list was found among his papers showing some of the causes for which he had crusaded—sweated industries, child labor, minimum wage, labor exchanges, slum clearance, prison reform, woman's suffrage, divorce law reform, caging of wild birds, ponies in mines, docking of horses' tails. During the World War he made it his rule to live on less than half his income, giving the rest to relief of war sufferers. He kept that rule, supporting peace work until the close of his life. When he received the Nobel Prize, he converted the $45,000 into a trust fund for the benefit of the P. E. N. Club and its work for international amity.

"He was a deeply religious man who believed in God and made it his fundamental motive to put life into harmony with the Divine Plan," Mrs. Galsworthy explained quietly. "He wanted to bring more beauty into life until reason and proportion should govern the behavior of men."

We stood in the yellow room on the third floor, where

he wrote many of his best plays and stories. She showed me book shelves which held the collection of his writings in many editions and languages. But our conversation did not center on the enduring qualities of his literary work. Mrs. Galsworthy talked about the sections of the world which were dear to them, their friends, and their interests in human welfare.

As she spoke of their love for each other and humanity, I looked out the casement window over the gay colored flower gardens, the terraced lawn, and the ancient trees to the Sussex Downs, where Mr. Galsworthy rode so many times on his horse, with his English sheep dog by his side.

The last words that I had heard him speak came to my mind: "But once man starts forth to walk his life through in sun and in rain. We are all tramps, not knowing what the next day may bring, or where we will sleep when day is done. But if we keep our courage up, forget ourselves, add a little beauty to the world about us, look in the face of mystery and feel the presence of the Eternal, we shall do well, we shall do very well!"

---

2. "Bitter the Chast'ning Rod":
JAMES WELDON JOHNSON

Hey, nigger! Don't you know better'n to walk over a road whar white men's workin'?—and with an umbrella up?"

A worker in the road gang shouted at the young Atlanta University student. He was on his way home from the shanty church where he had been teaching the Negro children near Hampton, Georgia. It was a scorching hot day and he dared to break the traditions of the county and walk ıs a Negro with an umbrella held over his head! They stopped, spades in hand, mouths open, gaping at his audacity. Their eyes burned with scorn.

Later, when he had received his university degree and was teaching in a southern city, he turned into a bicycle shop. A half-dozen white men were standing about. A nondescript fellow said with a sneer, "What wouldn't you give to be a white man?" The remark cut him to the quick. The insolence of it rocked him. The crowd of loafers tittered. A hot retort surged to his lips, but he controlled himself and answered, "Let me see. I don't know just how much I would give. I'd have to think it over. But, at any rate, I am sure that I wouldn't give anything to be the kind of white man you are. No, I am sure I wouldn't; I'd lose too much by the change." The white man turned livid, then purple. The titter died. Johnson turned away.

His name was soon made secure in American letters by his poems and the popular and successful songs that he wrote with his talented brother, Rosamond. Honorary degrees came from a number of universities in recognition of his achievements in literature. He acted as United States consul in Venezuela and Nicaragua, and went on special missions to other South American countries. For some years he has served as professor in Fisk University and at New York University.

A woman from New York asked him to criticize an article she had written. He met her in a Jacksonville park. The conductor and motorman saw him leave the street car and join the woman. They rushed back to the city with the story that a Negro was meeting a white lady in the woods. A detachment of troops was sent with guns and dogs to capture him.

He sat quietly listening to the reading of her story, unsuspecting, while the crowd collected. When he stood up and moved from the park bench, they closed in upon him, shouting, "Kill the damn nigger! Kill the black son of a bitch!" They tore at his clothes. Terror stricken, unable to make himself heard, he sensed that they were determined to kill him.

At this point a military officer arrested him and took him with the woman and a trolley car filled with troops and hoodlums to the commanding officer of the provost guard. Here he was permitted to explain that the lady was "not legally white"; with her apparent Caucasian skin she was a Negress. With apologies, the prominent citizen of Jacksonville was released, after another close contact with death before a mob.

He refers to the cruel discriminations practised in the United States, "From the day I set foot in France, I became aware of the working of a miracle within me. I became aware of a quick readjustment of life. I was suddenly free; free from a sense of impending discomfort, insecurity, danger; free from the problem of the many obvious adjustments to a multitude of bans and taboos; free from special scorn, special tolerance, special condescension, special commiseration; free to be merely a man."

The Negro National Anthem takes on new meaning when we appreciate the background of its author, James Weldon Johnson.

Lift every voice and sing,
Till earth and heaven ring,
Ring with the harmonies of Liberty;
Let our rejoicing rise
High as the list'ning skies,
Let it resound loud as the rolling sea.
Sing a song full of the faith that the dark past has taught us,
Sing a song full of the hope that the present has brought us;
Facing the rising sun of our new day begun,
Let us march on till victory is won.

44

Stony the road we trod,
Bitter the chast'ning rod,
Felt in the days when hope unborn had died;
Yet with a steady beat,
Have not our weary feet
Come to the place for which our fathers sighed?
We have come over a way that with tears has been watered,
We have come treading our path through the blood of the
  slaughtered
Out from the gloomy past,
Till now we stand at last
Where the white gleam of our bright star is cast.

God of our weary years,
God of our silent tears,
Thou who hast brought us thus far on the way;
Thou who hast by Thy might,
Led us into the light,
Keep us forever in the path, we pray.
Lest our feet stray from the places, our God, where we met
  Thee,
Lest our hearts, drunk with the wine of the world, we for-
  get Thee;
Shadowed beneath Thy hand,
May we forever stand,
True to our God,
True to our Native land.

"Black America is called upon to stand as the protagonist
of tolerance, of fair play, of justice, and of good will," Professor Johnson affirms. "Until white America heeds, we
shall never let its conscience sleep. For the responsibility
for the outcome is not ours alone. White America cannot
save itself if it prevents us from being saved. . . .

"In the situation into which we are thrown, let each one
of us, let the whole race, be ceaselessly on guard against the
loss of spiritual integrity. So long as we maintain *that* in-

tegrity we cannot be beaten down, not in a thousand years. For instance, we suffer the humiliations of Jim-Crowism; but we are not vitally injured so long as we are not Jim-Crowed in soul. . . .

"The pledge to myself which I have endeavored to keep through the greater part of my life is:

"I will not allow one prejudiced person or one million or one hundred million to blight my life. I will not let prejudice or any of its attendant humiliations and injustices bear me down to spiritual defeat. My inner life is mine, and I shall defend and maintain its integrity against all the powers of hell!"

---

3. Spirit Versus Force:

STEFAN ZWEIG

I MET Stefan Zweig in the seventeenth-century Capuchin monastery on top of the mighty Kapuzinerberg in Salzburg, Austria. He has made his home there for some years, within the quiet of ancient cloister walls. The alert doctor of philosophy had come in from a tramp in the hills. He welcomed me to his tea table, and we started to talk about the World War.

It was the war that brought Zweig to himself. Up to that time he had been the learned traveler, wandering from country to country, exploring Europe, Asia, Africa, and portions of the New World. Born in Vienna in 1881, he grew up in a comfortable Jewish family and was given a thorough education. Before leaving the university he published two volumes of poetry and established himself as the translator of Verhaeren, Verlaine, and other modern poets.

46

"Yes," he answered, "I did revolt against the World War. Fortunately I was moved from active service and escaped some of the suffering that tortured me at the front. Deadly days, they suffocated all free thought! That is why I wrote my symbolic play, *Jeremiah*. I had to cloak my revolt in the form of poetic figures, or the censors would have made away with me and my manuscript. I retold the story of Jeremiah, pointing out the everlasting road of suffering upon which militarism drives its slaves. I mentioned in the preface to the new American edition that the next generation will find it hard to realize the torment of the minority in those days. We lived amid liars who shouted their inanities day and night in thousands of newspapers, while those who loved justice and peace were despised and persecuted. Jeremiah, brave adversary of war, was a martyr for his convictions. That allegory was a protest from the German side. The play was given in Zurich in 1917, and then forgotten until the lunacy of war days abated. I stand by that protest and know now that I was in the right.

"Yes, the war brought me to with a start. My views of life were shattered. I had to rebuild everything, to grow into larger truth."

"Do you feel now that we have learned the lesson of war?"

"I am despondent. The light of liberalism is flickering. There are too many hot-headed jingoists clamoring for the place of leadership. There are still too few peace lovers in Europe! Peace has become a new catchword that diplomats use glibly, but they do not sense its demands; they are unwilling to pay its price."

"Is that true everywhere, Dr. Zweig?"

"Well, I have just come from Russia, to me the most interesting country in the world today. They are tackling an unparalleled enterprise."

"The people there are happy, do you think?"

"Not exactly happy, but they seem to be conscious that they are struggling together for a future ideal. Perhaps, in a way, they are like the Pilgrims who went from England to the New World, toiling, suffering for a better state that will come into being, at least for their children. It is heartening to find a people who talk of something beside the outgrown shibboleths of nationalism. . . .

"Now, let me ask you a question about America. Do you still have the Negro problem in the United States? Why should that particular prejudice exist in such acute form in your country, which is strong for equality? Europeans find it hard to understand."

I regretted that it still existed. My keen-minded host sparkled, his black eyes flashing.

"Don't let me sound unfair to America. You have more of the happy, free spirit over there than we do in Europe. No one over here would stop a motor car to pick up a pedestrian. He would have to know the traveler's standing and pedigree before he would even salute him. There are haunting suspicions everywhere in this old world, and that is unhealthy. . . .

"No, I am afraid religion has exerted a pretty shabby influence in these days. The church was quite solidly behind the war, preaching 'Die for the Fatherland and you will please your Father in heaven.' It has been a sorry record since the war, the story of too much patriotism!

"I try to grapple with a thought about the new religion in my study called *The Triumph of the Spirit*. The religion of self-content is too stifling. Happiness is not an adequate goal for life. We must live with the citizens of our world, and strive with them and give ourselves for the good of humanity. Although the fight is uncertain, we must be in it. How can any man be worth a million dollars today? Who could rise to such wealth without crushing a fellow being? . . . Only that poet can be necessary to our times who makes the rhythm of his poetry the echoed rhythm of living things, who takes into his quivering veins the life blood of a world in need!"

My train thundered back to Munich in the darkness. I took up the symbolic play of the popular biographer and novelist, and read by the flickering lights of a third-class car these words from the prophet Jeremiah, who pleaded with his people to resist war:

"I say unto you that war is a fierce and evil beast, one that devours the flesh of the strong and sucks the marrow of the mighty, crushing towns in its jaws and trampling the land beneath its hoofs. Those who awaken it shall not again lay it to sleep; and he who draws the sword will perish by the sword."

The people who had been stirred by propaganda argued with Jeremiah, "But ours is a holy war, a war of God waged in the everlasting name of our nation, a war of God, a war of God."

Jeremiah answered, "Couple not God's name with war. Not God makes war, but man. No war is holy; no death is holy; life alone is holy! . . . Peace is not a thing of weakness. It calls for heroism and action. Day by day you must wrest it from the mouths of liars. You must stand alone against the multitude; for clamor is always on the side of the many, and the liar has ever the first word. The meek must be strong; those who desire peace are continually at war."

The people repudiated him. War was declared, months of suffering followed. Jerusalem faced starvation. Jeremiah went to the king and told him to humble himself in order to save his people from death. The king refused, and the conflict dragged on until Jerusalem fell and its people were led away into captivity. Jeremiah journeyed with them, reminding them that it was not enough to believe in the flags and armies of a nation.

As the prophet and his comrades marched down the "everlasting road" into exile, a Babylonian soldier marveled at their courage. He said to his captain, "See, they are walking to meet the sun. His light shines on their foreheads, and they themselves shine with the strength of the sun. Mighty must their God be."

"Their God?" the captain answered, "Have we not broken down his altars? Have we not conquered him?"

The soldier murmured, "Who can conquer the invisible? Men we may slay, but the God who lives in them we cannot slay. A nation can be controlled by force; its spirit, never!"

---

4. Friend of the Lowly:

CHARLES F. ANDREWS

It was on a Christmas morning in India. The church was filled with native people. The young white man, a teacher who had come recently from England, felt an overwhelming spirit of good will toward those who crowded about him. Following a stirring hymn of the Nativity, the Athanasian creed was given out. He heard the choir boys in their white surplices recite in Urdu the old words, "Which faith except everyone do keep whole and undefiled, without doubt he shall perish everlastingly." It was crudely offensive on the day of good will toward men. The young clergyman drew back with revolt. Why should his faith, a white man's religion, condemn to hell the uncounted multitudes of India?

The rebellion of Charles F. Andrews led him beyond the creeds of his church to a broader fellowship of service and brotherhood that has made him perhaps the most beloved white man in India and has won him the title of Deenabandhu, friend of the lowly. In his undergraduate days in England he had gone to the college mission in Walworth, in the south-east side of London, and found among the slum people his first real convictions. He left Cambridge for a time and went as a lay worker to a poverty-stricken section in north England, where he tried to live on the same scale as the shipyard laborers. He returned to the East End of London to engage in settlement work, and then, at the age of thirty-three, set out for India.

He celebrated a second birthday as he stepped onto Indian soil, for he discovered the demand for a larger thought of God and for a wider human brotherhood. He followed Mahatma Gandhi to South Africa, where he fought for the uplift of indentured Indian laborers who had been taken to Africa under false pretenses and held there as virtual slaves. One morning, while walking with Gandhi, he saw an Indian laborer crouching along the road near some sugar cane. He crept up and touched Mr. Gandhi's feet as he pointed to unhealed wounds upon his back, inflicted by a beating. He pleaded for protection. When the trembling laborer saw that Andrews was white, he started back in terror. The frenzy of fear upon that brown face haunted the young clergyman for days, and made him swear that he would give his life to check race discrimination.

He preached one morning in a South African church. His friend, Gandhi, came to hear him. The white vestrymen turned him away with the curt words, "No colored men allowed here." "In that refusal," said Andrews vehemently to me years afterward, as if the betrayal still burned in his breast, "was the denial of Christ himself. . . ." "We soon found," he went on, "that the root of the tragedy in Africa was the color question. I sensed at last that it was impossible to observe racial discriminations in life once one had accepted the Christian philosophy. It was bound to lead to a class system, and that is wholly contrary to Christ's fundamental precepts, the fatherhood of God and the brotherhood of man."

Mr. Andrews spoke with quiet passion to us, his slight body bent forward, his bearded face lined with marks of suffering. He could not remain in a church that clung to creeds of condemnation and refused to share with men of all races. He searched years for truth—sharing the cave of the mystic St. Francis of modern India, Sundar Singh, barefoot friend of the poor; ministering to the lepers with the American, Samuel Stokes, who founded the Brotherhood of the Imitation of Jesus; giving up his possessions; living a homeless, celibate life among the lowliest people.

He sat at the feet of Rabindranath Tagore, poet-philosopher, and served as a voluntary worker in the school in the village of Santiniketan, the abode of peace. Three rules were inscribed upon the boundaries of this *ashram,* or retreat: No image shall be set up for worship. No life of man or animal shall be destroyed within its precincts. No controversy about religion shall be carried on. Men and women of every race and creed are welcome if they abide by these precepts.

One day during the summer holidays, Mr. Andrews fell ill with Asiatic cholera. No doctor was available until the next morning. Tagore hurried back from Calcutta and nursed his English friend with his own hands, until he was convalescent and able to be moved to a mountain hospital.

In association with Gandhi, Singh, Stokes, Tagore, and other leaders of India, the seeker from the West developed a new religion of universal sympathy and direct action. White men have smiled at him as they have seen him walk along a city street, with Mr. Tagore, carrying his Indian friend's suit case. No doubt white and brown men alike have called him a fool as they have observed him digging latrines in a cholera-infected village.

If you would locate "friend-of-the-lowly" Andrews, go to the scene of the most recent disaster—plague, flood, earthquake, or famine—and you will likely find him there. He is one of the first to serve. He considers it a privilege to share life with the needy. When cholera recently ravaged a Bengal town, he organized nursing squads and went to save as many people as he could. He staggered through swollen streams, carrying villagers to improvised hospitals made of bamboo and grass. He demanded that the high-caste neighbors who were too pious to touch their low-caste brothers should roll up their sleeves and serve as he served. When the most beloved white man in India talks, he speaks quietly, but he is so adept at showing people how that they are compelled to follow his example!

---

5. A Cup of Cold Water:

MOTOICHIRO TAKAHASHI

THEY CALLED the Japanese teacher "the father of the destitute unemployed." For months he lived in the Tokyo slums. He put up tents to shelter the homeless people. As "the mayor of the tent village" he doled out food to the wretched people. Most of the time there was little to give them except rice dough and potato peelings, with one blanket apiece for a bed, and for warmth a small charcoal fire. Most remarkable of all, the mayor of the tent village got a majority of the down-and-outers to pledge themselves to abstain from drinking and gambling. Many of them had families in the rural districts, and were struggling desperately to find work in the city and to provide for their children. The leader rebuilt the shattered lives of unemployed men who were living in cellars and caves. After sharing the sufferings of these derelicts, the young teacher wrote a play about his experiences, which ran in one of the Tokyo theaters and was broadcast throughout the Empire. People asked, "Who is this strange mayor of the tent village?" His name was Motoichiro Takahashi.

He had been a professor in a Japanese college. Claiming to be a Christian, he stated that he was a champion of peace and an enemy of war. In this college the students were required to take military training. Professor Takahashi protested against compulsory education in the technique of war in an institution dedicated to the ideals of peace. He not only protested, but he gave up his position and dedicated his life to work for peace education. This action called for courage at a time when patriotism and loyalty to the military system were very strong. A few months before his resignation, one of his school mates, a newly elected member of the Diet, had been assassinated by reactionaries who opposed his international ideas. Takahashi said he would seek revenge for his friend's death like a Christian: he began to live on thirty yen a month, giving bread to the poor, living on the top floor of a tenement house in the Fukugawa slums.

Without capital, without an organization, an office, or any paid helpers, he initiated his work among the children of Japan. He organized friendship clubs among school children, showing them how to collect foreign stamps and write letters to children of other countries. He believed youth could break the barriers of nationalism and build the world mind. Hundreds of young people wrote to him, sending in Japanese stamps and asking for foreign stamps. They said they wanted to know what American and European stamps looked like, since they had never seen any. One primary school boy in the country reported that he and five of his friends had organized a "World Peace Society." The tireless worker went to churches and temples throughout the islands, enlisting young people and building up scores of "International Children's Friendship Clubs."

He wrote plays and stories for the newspapers. His pen was active in creating poems to widen the horizon of his people and to spread ideas of international good will. He said, "The communists talk about an International made up of all the peoples of the world. We Christians must hold up an even bigger program—the Christian International which will bind all nations in the struggle to destroy war and establish peace!"

When Japan sent her military forces to attack Shanghai, Takahashi wrote these lines demanding peace, and addressed them to the Japanese Emperor:

Sublimely shine the stars in the eternal sky,
Living in this wonderful universe,
Yet killing one another!
What is your name, Yamato!*
Yamato, the great "Peace Nation". . . .
Are you not ashamed to acknowledge your name?

Broken in body by his sacrifices to help the poor and to outlaw war, Takahashi fell ill with tuberculosis, and after a few months of anguish, died in a Salvation Army sanitarium.

The intrepid idealist had given away everything he possessed. Devoted friends came to him. "What may we bring you?" they proffered, as they watched him suffer with Spartan courage.

---

* Poetic name for Japan, also meaning peace.

"A cup of cold water," was his answer. His throat tormented him.

The only material comfort he craved was the momentary release that cold water brought. He had already turned away from the luxuries of life. The fire of devotion burned brighter in his luminous eyes while his body grew more feverish and emaciated. . . .

Friends have set up a little shrine in his memory. Before his portrait they place each day a cup of cold water, and remember the unflinching good will of this obscure hero of the New Japan.

---

6. *Captain of the Pick-and-Shovel Brigade:*

PIERRE CERESOLE

I'M TIRED of all this talk!" The stalwart young Swiss spoke emphatically. "We have conference after conference on the peace of the world. Hundreds of folks sit about tables talking, but the world takes no notice. I will get twenty men and women to work with pick and shovel for peace, and perhaps somebody will pay attention!"

The son of a Cabinet member, and cousin of a major in the army who was hostile to pacifists, Pierre Ceresole declared himself to be a war resister. While serving a term in prison he determined that peace workers should be bound together into an aggressive fellowship with a morale like that of an army. He organized the Service Civil Volontaire International in 1920 with a small group of friends who were willing to work with their hands. This company made up of people from many nations proposed to go to any country in need and work there without pay under discipline like that of a military camp.

Their first job was a five months' project on one of the World-War battlefields, Esnes-Verdun, near Hill 304 and Dead Man's Hill. Ten volunteers restored a ruined and desolate sector by filling shell holes and preparing the fields for recultivation. They rebuilt a road, erected five barns, and left the place ready for human habitation. A German who helped in this strange mission said, "For a long time I have hoped for a chance to go and repair in France a little of what my brother—killed at Verdun—and his comrades were forced under military orders to destroy."

A few months later the rugged Swiss in his blue overalls appeared in Liechtenstein. The village of Schaan had been swept by flood. The river had burst over the dam and swept away bridges, homes, and barns in the valley. The villagers were busy repairing their houses when Pierre arrived. He saw the fertile fields buried under mud and stones. His call was answered by volunteers from twenty-two different nations.

The village school house and the theater were turned into quarters for the pick-and-shovel workers. A bugle awakened them at four-thirty in the morning. They breakfasted at five and went to work at five-thirty. Among the women volunteers were teachers, clerks, nurses, dressmakers; among the men were doctors, lawyers, musicians, students. They built a railway and moved sand and boulders from the fields until they uncovered the fertile soil. After nine hours at their toil, they swam in the Rhine, ate their evening meal, and joined in an international song fest.

The puzzled natives had never seen anything like the Volunteers. "Who are you, anyway?" they would ask.

"The International Volunteers."

"Well, who sent you here?"

"Why, no one. Pierre Ceresole called us, and we came."

"What else do you do? Do you fight?"

"No. We never destroy. We build!"

In six months the buried soil had been reclaimed and plowed for planting. The Volunteers dispersed.

Two years later came a flood in Lagarde, in southern France. Pierre went to hear the story at first hand: Two hundred people drowned. Roads buried, homes and orchards torn away, fields lost under debris.

The mayor of Lagarde received the peace leader. "Alas, we have no money to pay you!"

"We work without pay."

The mayor was amazed.

"Could you give us lodging and food?" asked Pierre.

The mayor led him to an old chateau that had withstood the flood. "How would this be? And we will allow you money to buy necessary provisions."

Two hundred and fifty workers arrived from Russia, Germany, England, America, and India. Six hundred more would have come if there had been quarters for them. For weeks they struggled to clean up the ruin of demolished buildings and the wreckage of the countryside. A power plant was rebuilt, bridges were erected, and roads laid out. When the summer's work was ended, the Volunteers had fed themselves so economically that they were able to turn back to the commune some seventeen hundred francs from their food allowance.

The villagers gathered to pay thanks to the workers. Their spokesman said, "You have made us see that nation can stand by nation. Your living example will make us readier in our turn to help others."

Their appreciation was expressed in 1931. Pierre and his workers were at work in a mining town, Bryn Mawr in Wales. Unemployment had brought desolation to the village. Its jobless citizens tried to occupy their empty time by clearing up the community. There were coal dumps, rubbish heaps, swamps. For two years the local men had worked; and then the Volunteers came to encourage them and complete the task.

The people of Lagarde sent a communication, and with it a gift of seventeen hundred francs: "To enable you to continue to do useful work as in the past, and to crown your patient efforts with prompt success, the Commune of Lagarde returns you the sum refunded. Good courage, friends, we are with you. You can count on us." The mayor came to the ceremonies at the dedication of the new Bryn Mawr with its coal dumps transformed into swimming pools and parks, its dirty streets lined with freshly white-washed cottages and blooming flowers.

With the Indian earthquake of 1934, Pierre Ceresole sounded another call for help and assembled his Volunteers amid the steaming fields of India. They set to work with the peasants to build breakwaters, drain fields, and move villages to higher land.

To the founder of the Volunteers it was just another demonstration of good will. With back aching from shoveling in the burning sun, but with heart undaunted, he wrote to friends in Europe, "We intend to build a bridge across oceans of hate and misery, but to begin with we are making a path across a marsh where one wets one's feet. Still, we have made a beginning!"

---

7. Awakener of Millions:

HU SHIH

THE MASTER is dead," the tragic word was brought to the young widow and her child. The little mother, who was left alone in the world with a four-year-old son, could not read or write, but she was determined to educate her boy to be a scholar. He was a small, weak lad, but she poured out her love for him. She would waken him in the morning and explain to him how fine a man his father was and what great hopes he had cherished for his son. At the age of eight the boy was reading Chinese and learning the classics. The mother made a tremendous sacrifice when she decided to send him to Shanghai. He studied in the city for six years. Mrs. Hu spent all her money. The disheartened student was desperate. He would have to give up his plans. He tried to lose his despair in dissipation. But at length he journeyed to the capital, to make a final effort. There he won a scholarship that sent him to America.

For seven years he remained in the United States. He returned to his homeland in 1917 as Dr. Hu Shih, having received a doctorate in philosophy at Columbia University. The features he liked best in Western life were optimism and effort, and he carried them into his program for a new China. The young philosopher joined the Revolutionists and soon was a leader of literary and social reform. He battled for a new type of literature that was written in the language of the people and not in abstract, old-fashioned style. He said the old philosophy, which made China content with things as they were, had to be replaced by interest in progress.

As a pioneer in the Renaissance Movement, which has brought tremendous changes in China during the past twenty years, Dr. Hu wrote: "The fundamental meaning of the Renaissance is a new attitude. It may be called the critical attitude. This means a reclassifying of what is good and what is not good. This means we must question traditional customs. Do they justify their existence? Are the ideas of the ancient sages correct today? Should we follow what the majority of the people believe, doing things in the traditional manner, or can we find better ways? We need a re-evaluation of all values. Formerly we thought that women should bind their feet to increase their beauty, but now we regard this custom as a tragedy. A few years ago the family host served opium to his guests, while today its use is prohibited by law. We need to re-evaluate all values."

Today Hu Shih is called the "Father of the Chinese Renaissance." His books are read by thoughtful people throughout China. Although still in his forties, he has been a hero for fifteen years. He has become the voice of a new day. For example, fifteen years ago he issued his demand for the freedom of women. "Certain steps are necessary to free Chinese women: The rigid old family system must be altered until there is respect for each individual. The old law which said, 'While at home a woman must obey her father, when married she must obey her husband, when her husband dies she must obey her son,' must go. There should be no difference between sexes. Women must be given the opportunity to make a living so they can be independent. The use of women as slaves and concubines must be prohibited."

Dr. Hu once spoke to a group of us who were teaching in China. After dinner in a Peiping restaurant he made some disturbing prophecies about coming turmoil between the East and the West. Three years later China was driving out the white man and revolting against the Western imperialism that was being imposed upon her. Hu Shih welcomed Western civilization but scorned the religious and nationalistic bigotries of the Occident.

As a champion of the practical, he summons China to awake to new ways. He says, "I am tired of this talk about the Orient being more spiritual than the Occident. In reality the Occident is more spiritual because it concerns itself with the uplift of people. Western people work for freedom, equality, and justice. Eastern people sit and quietly repeat the name of Buddha. In the Orient there is too much passive acceptance of poverty, the desire to please heaven, and endurance of things as they are. In the Occident there is dissatisfaction with poverty, unwillingness to endure wrong, determined struggle, and continuous improvement of the environment. China must make her religion practical and active. Her people must think in terms of human needs and work for progress!"

---

8. He Could Not Forget the Underdog:

ANTHONY ASHLEY COOPER, LORD SHAFTESBURY

ANTHONY ASHLEY COOPER, eldest son of the Earl of Shaftesbury, was born in 1801 on a country estate in Dorset. His father was heartless to the farm tenants and to his children. His mother, interested only in fashion, felt no concern for her boy. He was shipped off to school when he was seven, a lonely lad who had never known affection. "Nothing could have surpassed the school for filth, bullying, neglect, and hard treatment of every sort," he wrote in later years. "Nor had it in any respect any one compensating advantage, except perhaps, it may have given me an early horror of oppression and cruelty." The only friend of his childhood was a household servant, Maria Mills. She gave him some love and a religious faith that stayed with him through the eighty-four years of his life.

At twelve he went to Harrow. Another indelible impression was made here when he saw a pauper's funeral. Shocked by the scene, he made a resolve to give his life to the poor. He was graduated from Oxford and went to the House of Commons when he was twenty-five. His marriage to Lady Emily Cooper was the turning point of his career. "Marriage, I have seen, corrects many and various errors in a man's character." This confession came from an early happiness that endured through the years.

Lord Shaftesbury was made a minister at twenty-six, but that was the only office he was to hold during a long public career except for a short term of a few months under Peel. Although he was not to be a minister or party leader, he became a dominant force in the reconstruction of English life. Through his courage and persistent effort he established a record as one of England's greatest humanitarians.

Before Lord Shaftesbury's factory reform bill, children were entirely unprotected except in cotton mills, and in those mills children of nine could be made to work twelve hours a day. In 1835 there were 220,000 workers in cotton mills: 28,000 were children under thirteen, 27,000 boys between thirteen and eighteen, 106,000 girls or women over thirteen, and 58,000 men over eighteen.

One witness, an overseer in a flax mill in Dundee, said that there were nine workers in the room under his charge who had begun work before they were nine years old, and that six of them were splay-footed and the other three deformed in other ways. A tailor at Stanningley, who had three daughters in the mill, described the life of his household: In the ordinary time the hours were from six in the morning to half-past eight at night; in the brisk time, for six weeks in the year, these girls, the youngest of them "going eight," worked from three in the morning to ten and half-past ten at night.

Lord Shaftesbury agitated in Parliament and in public

for years—speaking, writing, educating—until he succeeded in carrying through the first factory reform bills. Public indifference and the hostility of vested interests almost defeated him. At the age of forty he was a poor man with a large family. He was so absorbed in social reforms that he gave scant consideration to his own business affairs. His father had disinherited him, at least cut off all support; he had no sympathy with his son's idealism.

Most men in public life inherited wealth or possessed some substantial income. Cobden's friends gave him £120,000 during his career. Pitt left debts of £40,000 at his death. Lord Shaftesbury could not even employ a typist, but had to do all his letters by hand. Serving on commissions, he was forced to make his own statistical studies after visiting factories, mines, and asylums, and write his own reports and addresses. Some friends advised him to give up politics and find a secure living for himself. His reply was a vigorous effort to reform the coal mines.

In many of the mines children were employed at five and six years to push cars of coal in passages only eighteen inches high. They were harnessed to carts like dogs and pulled coal cars on their hands and knees. Bound as apprentices from the age of eight and nine for a twelve-year period, they worked not less than twelve hours a day. The passing of the Mines Act of 1842 was Lord Shaftesbury's most striking personal achievement. It was the beginning of better conditions for mine workers.

He retired from Parliament in 1846, his interest being absorbed in philanthropic work. He went to the London slums and was appalled by conditions there. He demanded that something should be done about the filth, disease, and hunger of the people, crying, "Oh, if some Dives would give me two or three hundred pounds, the price of a picture or a horse, I could set up schools to educate six hundred wretched children!" Unable to justify the luxury of the upper level of society, he wrote, "I have two rooms to myself and two fires. I deplore the waste of fuel when there are so many who have none. This feeling is growing upon me, and may degenerate into stinginess, or, at least, a parsimony in the exercise of just hospitality. The amount of waste in all things is prodigious; in some instances careless; in some inevitable. Why, the very crumbs and scrapings of finished dishes in a thousand well-fed families would, week by week, sustain a hundred persons!"

He championed better housing and public health. During the Crimean War, Florence Nightingale received more help from him than from any one in England in her fight against the ravages of battle and cholera. When he came into his own property in 1851 he discovered scandals on his father's estate. "I have passed my life in rating others for allowing rotten houses and immoral, unhealthy dwellings; and now I come into an estate rife with abominations!" he exclaimed. "Why, there are things here to make one's flesh creep; and I have not a farthing to set them right!" He took up the cause of the agricultural laborers.

Early in his career the status of the treatment of the insane came before Parliament. The young man was a member of the investigating committee. At one establishment in Bethel Green four hundred cases were shut up together with no attempt to cure them except for the visit of a doctor for an hour or two every other day. The keepers were unwilling to show the infirmary, it was in such a bad condition. The more violent were called "crib-room cases" and were placed in boxes six feet long, covered with straw, and chained by the arms and legs. Fifteen of these cases spent the night in a room twenty-six feet long. They were left for the week-end without attention. Monday morning they were led into the court yard and plunged into cold water to rid them of the vermin and filth in which they had been lying.

Lord Shaftesbury served for years on various commissions for the supervision and reform of the lunacy laws. He wrote of his investigations: "One of the first rooms that we went into contained nearly a hundred and fifty patients, in every form of madness, a large proportion of them chained to the wall, some melancholy, some furious, but the noise and din and roar were such that we positively could not hear each other; every form of disease and every form of madness was there. I never beheld anything so horrible and so miserable. Turning from that room we went into a court, appropriated to the women. In that court there were from fifteen to twenty women, whose sole dress was a piece of red cloth, tied about the waist with a rope, covered with filth; they were crawling on their knees, and it was the only place where they could be."

The reforms in the lunacy laws which he carried through Parliament remained in effect until after his death, when more liberal provisions were adopted.

In 1873 Lord Shaftesbury drew attention in the House of Lords to the lot of the chimney sweeps. He had been chairman of the Climbing Boys' Society, created years before for the protection of boys in this trade. A lad of ten was discovered who had been sold five times to different masters. Crippled by injuries so that he was unable to walk, he was still forced to do as many as twelve chimneys a day. The Society informed the public of the boys who were burned to death, tortured, and crippled by being forced into flues. It was found that masters who employed these lads hardened the flesh of the boys by rubbing their elbows and knees with strong brine, close by a hot fire. When they returned from work with arms and legs bleeding, the master would threaten them with a cane and administer more brine to their wounds. Six was considered "a nice trainable age" for the climbing boy to begin.

Hearing of the suffocation and death of a seven-year-old boy in a flue at Gateshead, Lord Shaftesbury made a plea for action. His wife was on her death bed at this time. Three years later he secured legislation which put an end to these scandals.

There were "ragged schools" for the slum children and a multitude of other interests to consume the last energies of the tireless reformer, who fought for the rights of his fellowmen until he fell asleep in his eighty-fourth year.

----

9. "Power to Act Is Duty to Act":

PETER KROPOTKIN

TAKE Makar with this note to the police station, and let a hundred lashes with the birch rod be given him!" This was the order that young Prince Kropotkin received from his father. Makar, the butler, had disobeyed, and a serf could be punished at the will of his owner.

Peter was terrorized at the thought of the servant's beating. He waited with trembling in the dark corridor until the sobbing butler returned. He was ashamed of his father. He felt the burden of such injustice upon him; and he prayed that he might save the serfs from their misery. When Makar passed him in the hallway, Peter seized his hand and kissed it. The man jerked his hand away and cried, "Let me alone; you, too, when you are grown up, will you not be the same?" Peter cried, "No, never!"

The young man kept his word. From that time he lived

to show that the serf as well as his master had a soul. Because he cared, his whole life was given to free the Russian masses. He reasoned, "What right had I to these highest joys, when all around me was nothing but misery and struggle for a moldy bit of bread? Knowledge is power. Men must know. What if knowledge should become the possession of all? The masses want to know; they are willing to learn; they can learn."

Kropotkin grew up in a wealthy Russian home. He was educated in the pages' corps in the court of Alexander II. When his studies were completed, he surprised his associates by choosing service in Siberia in preference to military life. Parades and court balls did not appeal to him; he thought of the scientific exploration and the social reforms that he might achieve in the great north country. Alexander II spoke to the young graduates before they went off on their terms of duty. He seemed to forget his liberalism and repudiate the reforms he had suggested: "If any of you —which God preserve you from—should under any circumstances prove disloyal to the Czar, the Throne, and the Fatherland, take heed of what I say—he will be treated with all se-veri-ty of the laws, without the slightest com-mi-se-ra-tion!" The Czar's face was full of the expression of blind rage.

Peter saw the foreboding sign. He muttered to himself, "Reaction, full speed backwards. The Czar is a used-up man; he is going to give it all up." The five years in Siberia brought genuine education in life and human character. He was stationed at Chita, explored the Amur River country, resided at Irkutsk, studied the geography of Manchuria, and made an investigation of economic conditions among the Ussuri Cossacks. He returned to St. Petersburg for five years of study in mathematics and geography. He served as secretary to the Russian Geographical Society and made explorations in Finland and Sweden. At thirty, Prince Kropotkin was an accomplished scholar in mathematics, geography, and art, a writer, musician, and a linguist who knew seven languages.

But he chose to give his life to social reform. He was distressed by the ebb of liberalism. "Where were the progressives?" he asked. "What had become of them?" He looked up some of them. They admonished, "Prudence, young man!" "Iron is stronger than straw." "One cannot break a stone wall with his forehead." He shuddered to see men giving up. In Switzerland he studied the International Workingmen's Association and affiliated himself with it. He became an active member of a little group of liberals. They were all under suspicion of the Czar's spies.

What would he do? Perhaps it was best to go to his father's estate and start a school, an experimental farm, or a co-operative enterprise through which he might help the masses. But that was impossible. The authorities would imprison him. He could only do a little for the weavers and cotton workers, and await opportunity.

One evening he gave a paper before the Geographical Society. On his way home his carriage was stopped and he was led to the fortress of Peter and Paul. For two years the prince awaited trial, confined in a dark room. The guards refused to speak to him, and he had no communication with his fellow-prisoners. He tried heroically to keep from going insane. He walked five miles a day in a cell that was ten steps wide, and practised gymnastic exercises with a stool. His brother, Alexander, brought him writing paper, and he completed his book on the glacial hypothesis. The courageous brother was exiled because he protested against the cruel treatment of the fortress, and twelve years later he died in Siberia.

After nearly two years in his cell, Peter Kropotkin fell ill with scurvy. The Grand Duke Nicholas, brother of the Czar, urged him to give up his liberal social views, but the champion of suffering Russia refused to leave his dungeon! Threatened with death, he was moved to the hospital. He recovered and was permitted to walk in the court yard under guard for a few minutes each day.

Friends planned his escape. When a violin played a mazurka from Kontsky, the prisoner was to throw off his dressing gown and run for the gate. He had been practising for days how to rid himself of the cumbrous garment, and trying daily to build enough energy into his weakened body to make the dash to the waiting carriage outside. Several attempts were futile. But at last all factors united favorably. He made the gate and flung himself into the carriage. The horse galloped down the street. Every carriage in that section had been rented by his friends, so that the guards could not pursue him.

He escaped to Finland, to Sweden, and then to England. But this release was but the beginning of a long life hounded and tormented by police. He was imprisoned for several years in Lyons and Clairvaux, France. He tried to dodge his ubiquitous enemies and continue his writing of books, editing of newspapers, and co-operation in reform movements.

His greatest work was *Mutual Aid*. He opposed the Darwinian theory that the story of life is solely a struggle for existence. Evolution, he believed, is the product of mutual aid and co-operative effort. "The fittest are the most social animals, and sociability appears as the chief factor of evolution.... The solitary being is wretched, restless, because he cannot share his thoughts and feelings with others. When we feel some great pleasure, we wish to let others know that we exist, we feel, we love, we live....

"It is the overflowing life that seeks to spread. Power to

act is duty to act. The moral obligation is the condition of the maintenance of life. The plant cannot prevent itself from flowering. Sometimes to flower means to die. Never mind, the sap mounts all the same. It is the same with the human being when he is full of force and energy. He expands his life. He gives without calculation, otherwise he could not live. If he must die like the flower when it blooms, never mind; the sap rises if the sap is there."

Prince Peter Kropotkin gave up vast estates to suffer the lot of a fugitive. Although we may not share the views he developed as an intellectual anarchist, we admire him because he lived what he preached, in simplicity, supporting himself by his scientific writing. Broken in health, an exile by choice, he refused to compromise. "Power to act is duty to act!"

---

10. Blue Prints for a Better World:
HERBERT GEORGE WELLS

You ask if we are going to have a United States of Europe?" My host, H. G. Wells, spoke with rapid-fire precision. "No! Never! Never a United States of Europe. It must be a United States of the World. The European countries cannot join unless the nations of the world do! It must be world wide. All nations must come into that new order where there is understanding of how we live and think as human beings, where there is a reconstruction of society on a new theory of economics and the teaching of history as it ought to be taught."

"Are we making any real progress?"

"On a small scale," he continued. "Financial, business, and scientific enterprises are outgrowing the old bounds and beginning to operate on an international scale. But the old traditions still hold. Pernicious influences are at work today. At any time we may have a flare-up. There are leaders who threaten to pursue the very follies that led to our last debacle. It may come in the same way and in about the same place. Germany, Italy, and other nations have their nationalist parties who clamor with suicidal chauvinism. A spark may at any time cause the great conflagration, a conflict far more deadly than the previous one."

His incisive and original comments proved a versatile acquaintance with contemporary events.

"Do you think it is true," I asked, "that England has demonstrated where she stands, and that it is now up to the United States to lead off in the outlawry of war?"

"Essentially, yes. It is a question of how much England can trust the United States. I am willing to bet sixty to forty, or even seventy to thirty, that the Americans will play fair with us; but as you know, all Americans cannot be trusted—you have those who do not think and who therefore are dangerous. There is a sinister element in the United States. Your commerce is remarkable, but it may prove to be short-sighted and may lead to a disastrous dénouement. America has failed to make full proof of the idealism she enunciated at the end of the war. Europe was deeply stirred by her sacrifice, but now realizes that some of these same Americans can demand a pound of flesh for every promise. In moments of sentimentalizing, the Americans have a way of tying up the other party in an inexorable business agreement. There has been a lamentable lack of co-operation between Great Britain and the United States. The united English-speaking people could have prevented the World War, or at least warded off its coming for a decade, but they failed to co-operate then. We should be one in united effort for all good things because we are brothers in culture and ideals. We must aim for that common relation. I have the hope that America will become less nationalistic and more of an international mind as your many diverse population groups are assimilated, extremes are burnt out, and the American conscience is developed."

The author of *An Outline of History,* which sold more than a million copies, the amazingly successful writer before me, was the son of an English housemaid and a gardener who had but one love, cricket. The first thirteen years of his life had been spent in a crockery shop where they eked out a miserable existence and tried to dodge ever-present debts. Here Herbert George suffered headaches and bilious attacks and discovered his love for books when he was laid up for weeks with a broken leg. He was apprenticed as a draper's assistant. At the University of London he took up the study of science, became a socialist, and wore a red tie. He was then a thin lad, five feet five inches tall, undernourished and pale, threatened with tuberculosis. He broke down in his first job as a teacher and suffered years of illness, hemorrhages of the lungs, and kidney trouble. Tuberculosis haunted him along with the specter of poverty. Until he was forty his sense of physical inferiority was a source of acute distress. He wrote for papers, school books, tried stories of every type, and after a long battle established himself as a man of letters.

"What medium can we use for nurturing the New Society, the Christian Church?" I said.

Looking at me with a twinkle in his eyes, Mr. Wells answered,

"Can you stomach the doctrine? I have always felt that Christianity has a lot of legend and superstition in it. Its heritage from Babylonian, Egyptian, and ancient rites might well have been dropped long ago. If I searched your person would I find lurking vestiges of the Trinity? Do we re-

73

quire the Christian ethic to create a new internationalism? Let us first teach history on the basis of historic facts, requiring that texts and teachers present world thought fairly. You Americans harp on Bunker Hill and make history center about it when it was really of rather small moment to an Englishman. A biological understanding of how we are constituted and how we are to live will eliminate many of the unfit and prevent abnormal mental trends. A new economics and social organization are of primary importance."

We turned from the tea table. "Will we ever check nationalism?" I asked.

"Nationalism is not an ancient loyalty. It is not instinctive like love of family. It is a new development, an artificially imposed concept. And here our hope lies. Human loyalties can be enlarged. We can expand to broader thoughts. In time we will create the mentality that will bring into being a United States of the World."

He handed me a paper-bound book as I said goodbye.

"Humanity can develop in co-operative living. In the space of a few centuries much progress has been made. There is still much that can and must be achieved."

The message of the little book is summed up in these words: "At bottom all human affairs are mental. At bottom all this danger of war, this immense preoccupation with war, rests on the narrow patriotic idea—the old-fashioned and out-of-date, narrow patriotic ideals. This is a very deeply rooted complex in the mind. But it is not an ineradicable complex. People are not born combatant patriots. Patriotism is put into them. It is talked into them. It is taught them. Flags are waved at them. But what is taught can to a certain extent be untaught. And teaching can be changed. Children can be taught that the conquest of knowledge, the establishment of world order, the attain-

74

ment of human health and happiness, are finer ends than pulling down and tearing up one flag in order to hoist another. Alter ideas and you alter the world.

"The price of world peace is the abandonment of the ideas of sovereign independence and national competition. We have to see to it that our children do not grow up fierce and intolerant patriots. We have to see that they grasp and are tuned to the new ideas and are no longer enslaved to the old. We need an education that will turn mankind from tradition to hope. There is no way to world peace except through these preliminary battles in the mind."

III
THEY CONQUERED OBSTACLES

1. *Two Selves Who Became One:*

ANNE SULLIVAN MACY
AND HELEN KELLER

THE MOTHER bathed the girl's eyes with geranium water and prayed to the Virgin Mary for her healing. They were too poor to take her to the doctor, and her neglected trachoma had caused partial blindness. The intemperate and incompetent Irish immigrant, her father, contended that all her sore eyes needed was a drop of water from the blessed river Shannon and they would be well.

Anne Sullivan's mother died when she was ten; and she was sent from her Springfield home with her crippled brother, Jimmie, to the state poor house at Tewksbury, Massachusetts. The shabby buildings of the state infirmary were crowded with a dismal group of social derelicts, most of them old people. The lonely children were placed with the adults and no provision was made for their education. Sanitary conditions were incredible. Seventy of the eighty foundlings received the year before had died, while out of the twenty-seven received the year of the coming of the Sullivans, not one had survived. Delirium tremens cases, the insane, and sufferers from contagious diseases were quartered together. Death came almost every day. There was a continual procession of cots to the death house. Fifty years later Anne Sullivan Macy could still hear the sounds of metal wheels clattering on the rough floor, bearing the dead away.

Her only friend, deformed Jimmie, soon died. "I crept to the side of his bed and touched him," she wrote. "Under the sheets I felt the little cold body, and something in me broke. My screams wakened everyone in the hospital. Someone rushed in and tried to pull me away; but I clutched the little body and held it with all my might. Another person came, and the two separated us. They dragged me back to the ward and tried to put me in bed; but I kicked and scratched and bit them until they dropped me upon the floor, and left me there, a heap of pain beyond words." She followed her brother to the death house; and the next day to his grave. There was no service, because the priest was sick.

"I sat down between my bed and his empty bed, and longed desperately to die. I believe very few children have ever been so completely left alone as I was. I felt that I was the only thing that was alive in the world. Not a ray of light shone in the great darkness which covered me that day."

When she was fourteen an investigator visited the almshouse. Anne ran to him. She pulled at his coat. "I want to go to school." He discovered that she was nearly blind and arranged for her to attend Perkins Institution for the Blind, in Boston. When she arrived she did not know how to spell or write her own name. She had no tooth brush, petticoat, hat, coat, or gloves. But she was a bright girl and made steady progress in her difficult studies.

While she was working in a boarding house one summer a friend took her to Dr. Bradford at the Massachusetts Eye and Ear Infirmary. There were two operations. Anne could see the Charles River, the windows in buildings; and she could thread a needle without using her tongue.

When she was scarcely twenty the young graduate received the offer of her first job, and began her life work as the other self of Helen Keller. The little Alabama girl was four. She had lost sight, hearing, and speech following a severe illness at nineteen months. There was no one who knew how to release her from her prison of darkness and silence. She was a serious problem, nervous, stubborn, revolting against the dark and lonely world in which she was shut up from all human contact.

Helen resisted Anne's efforts to embrace her on the day of her arrival, jerked the bag from her, and flew into a temper. The young tutor began with infinite patience the struggle to teach her pupil to eat quietly at the table, to fold her napkin, to dress herself. She had to take the child away from her parents to a cottage on the farm, and there strive alone to master the resolute will and win the affection of the wretched little girl. The battle called for stamina; but the teacher won and a friendship began that lasted over fifty years.

By the touch of her fingers in Helen's hand she revealed the mystery that things had names such as milk, mug, doll. In three weeks she knew eighteen nouns and three verbs and was asking what familiar objects were called. She also learned to feel Anne's throat speak words, sometimes reaching her fingers inside her teacher's throat until she gagged her. Months and years of patient guidance refined the brilliant mind of the girl who battled with three handicaps. The resourceful companion led her through Radcliffe College. Enticing offers came to Anne, but she would not desert her other self. Her own eyes caused her to suffer, but affliction tended to keep her closer to the mind that was dependent upon her.

They traveled together, speaking to vast audiences, appearing before courts and learned societies as Miss Keller became the world leader of the blind. Mrs. Macy's probing, liberal brain and her sympathy toward the lonely and underprivileged are reflected in the ideas of her pupil.

I heard Helen Keller answer the question, "What is the hardest thing you ever had to do?" with these words: "My hardest task was to learn to speak. My inability to speak and to hear have been worse handicaps than blindness. A new life came for me as I began to speak. Speech gives my spirit wings. These wings for me are broken, but they help me more quickly to reach the minds of others."

She stood by Mrs. Macy and said, "I cannot see the stars you see in the heavens tonight, but there are other stars just as bright that shine in my soul. Every day is full of meaning for me. There is much work for me to do. I have my friends, I ride horseback, I enjoy my dogs. I spend many happy moments in my flower garden. It is small but everything that I love is there in it—flowers, sunshine, and wind."

When Miss Keller visited Luther Burbank's famous gardens in Santa Rosa, California, she was able to distinguish every specimen except two plants.

"My limitations never make me unhappy," she explained. "I like to think that through my limitations God is working out some good purposes. My troubles have also been great adventures. They have brought me understanding, friendship, and taught me how to serve the world." Her face was touched with compassion as she urged her listeners to share the blessings of life with 174,000 blind fellow-Americans: "If you really want to help the blind you must realize that they are just as you would be if you had to live in the dark.

They have the same feelings that you have. They crave the same things—work, play, food, and pleasure. You have heard how a new life started for me when one little word from another touched the darkness of my mind. Help my comrades to awaken as I have awakened to the sunshine and beauty of life!"

Would the genius of Helen Keller ever have unfolded if it had not been for Anne Sullivan Macy, her other self?

---

2. "Remember Who You Are":

ROLAND HAYES

His parents had been slaves. When he was born in Curryville, Georgia, in 1887, they lived in a tiny cabin on a parcel of land that had been given them in an ex-slave settlement. His father died when Roland was twelve; his mother managed the plowing and planting as well as cooking and washing. The boys helped as they could, and tried to rent more land to raise crops on shares. There were a few months of school each year, with most of the time in the fields. Mrs. Hayes was penniless, with no schooling, but she had wisdom. She wanted to give her children an education, and determined to move them to Chattanooga.

Selling the crop, cow, and horse, they set forth for the city. Roland got a job in a window-weight factory. He was fifteen. It was his routine to unload scrap iron, build fires, carry ladles full of molten metal, and pour them into the casting molds. He cried at night with sore muscles. His legs and feet were burned by splatterings of hot iron. The scars will always be with him.

Promoted from an eighty-cents-a-day position, he became

foreman of the core department. The men liked him because he sang as he worked. Now and then he crowded in a few weeks of school. The church choir was an outlet for the melodies that were latent in his nature. One night at the church a young Negro music teacher named Arthur Calhoun, who had been studying at Oberlin, discovered Roland's voice. He took him to a white man's home and encouraged him to sing for a group of friends. Some of the white women left the room, but when they heard the rich voice of the iron worker they were lured back.

That evening the aspiring singer heard great voices for the first time on the gramophone—Caruso and Sembrich. "That night I was born again," the musician wrote. "It was as if a bell had been struck, that rang in my heart. And it has never ceased to ring there! I had not known what my friend meant when he talked of music. I had not been capable of imagining it. The revelation was so overwhelming that I was like one who had been born blind and suddenly is given sight."

Arthur Calhoun was thrilled, "You are put here in the world for a purpose, Roland. You must sing!"

The iron worker saved fifty dollars and set out for Oberlin College. Forced to stop in Nashville for a time, he found that his savings were exhausted. He heard of Fisk University in that city. He was accepted on one month's probation. His first job brought him lodging, food, and one dollar a week for spending money. He stayed on four years and was graduated.

The Fisk Jubilee Singers went to Boston in 1911. Roland went ahead of them to look about the city and see what his chances were for studying there. With Arthur Hubbard as teacher he worked as a bell hop and office messenger to provide his living and musical instruction. When a brother married, he brought his mother to live with him. It was a shabby, dark apartment. The student was able to buy one article, a stove. The beds, tables, and chairs were fashioned from packing crates and boxes.

After six years of study, a daring experiment was attempted, the first concert in Symphony Hall. The building had been rented without a cent. He typed the invitations and sold tickets in advance to pay the rent. His accompanist, Lawrence Brown, stood by faithfully. The curious audience was amazed by his Negro spirituals and his French, German, and Italian repertory. "It was more of a service than a concert," one critic wrote the next day.

While singing in California, he was asked a provocative question, "What is there in your singing that white artists do not possess?" Hayes was puzzled. "What did I know of myself, of my people? Here we are in America. We were lifted out of our old environment and set down here —aliens in body and soul. Shreds and tatters of our ancient qualities still cling to us, but what was the original fabric like?"

He set out for Africa to learn more of the Negro soul. But he got only as far as England. There he sang by royal command in Buckingham Palace and appeared at Wigmore Hall. He went into Germany while black troops were still quartered along the Rhine and overcame the German hostility through the rendition of Brahms and Schubert. There were triumphant concerts in Berlin and Vienna in 1923. In Paris he sang with the Cologne orchestra. The *Pravda* wrote of his concerts in Moscow: "The debut of Roland Hayes had to be the great event of the musical world of today, and truly it has proved itself the greatest. Out of every song with its deeply musical mood was born a feeling of wonder reaching such a high point in technique that we can speak of it only with the highest praise."

With the acclaim of the world the humble artist looks

back to the day he tramped along the dusty road from Curry-ville to Chattanooga, and the times he kicked off his loose-fitting shoes onto the foundry floor when hot drops of iron splashed angrily on him. The melodies were then singing in his soul. "I knew, then, that my voice was given me by God Almighty for some high purpose, not to make me great, but to serve my people. I was His instrument, that I knew, but how He wanted to use me I had to find out. I am beginning to understand. The Negro has a contribution to make to art. The spirituals, which the white man recognizes as art, are only a beginning of what we can do. What else there is for us to give to the world we cannot know until we begin to fashion it. We are free, we have access to all the knowledge in the world. So far, practically everything has been done for us by the white race. The rest we must do ourselves!"

The wisdom of his faithful advisor, his mother, is summed up in the words that she has repeated to him through the days of struggle and success, "Remember who you are!"

Winner of the Spingarn medal, scholar, artist, genuine and genial friend, Roland Hayes still believes in his moral mission. "There is a purpose and plan in my life in that I shall help my people to use what has been given them; that I shall have my share in rediscovering the qualities we have almost let slip away from us; and that we shall make our special contribution—only a humble one perhaps, but our very own, to human achievement!

"Money, reputation, influence, these mean nothing to me personally. I say this with sincerity. I know why they have come to me, and how I am to use them. I look back over the past twenty years, during which I have been led on, step by step; and I can see now the purpose behind every struggle that gave me strength and courage, every thought that stead-ied me, every contest that gave me human understanding!"

This artist who has come up from slavery bought the old Georgia plantation from the southern family who once "owned" his mother. Every year now he slips away from his Boston home and his concert tours to work for a time on the farm there, helping his fellow Negroes to reach out after the education which can bring them a new world.

A mother's words still guide him. Elated by his invitation to sing in Buckingham Palace, he sent her years ago an enthusiastic cablegram. She wired in reply, "Remember who you are!"

----

3. "Truth Will Prevail":
TOMAS G. MASARYK

In the year 1863 a peasant lad of thirteen was working in a village blacksmith shop in Moravia. His father, a coachman, and his mother, a domestic cook, were poor and humble people, but they had sent their son to the village school. Being one of the imperial serfs, the father found difficulty in obtaining permission to send the boy on to secondary school. When provision was made, he went off to high school dressed in a made-over coachman's suit. Here he showed an aptitude for mechanics, and was therefore brought home and apprenticed to a neighbor, the local blacksmith.

The boy at the anvil, Tomas G. Masaryk, enjoyed his work, but did not give up hope for an education. When he was not pounding iron he could be found in a corner of the shop devouring a book. Fate might have kept him in the smithy had it not been for a visit of Professor Luduik, his

84

old piano teacher. Tomas was ashamed to greet the dignified gentleman because he was so blackened with smoke and soot. He ran home to hear his mother report that the professor's father wanted him to serve as teaching assistant, without pay, but with the privilege of study. He spent two years as rector's assistant, and then made his way to the University of Vienna, where he developed into a brilliant student of philosophy and a lecturer on the faculty.

At the age of thirty-two he was called to the University of Prague in his homeland. He won popularity as a teacher. Young people admired him because he was democratic and outspokenly fearless. His American wife had helped him to become world-minded. He was a challenging teacher and writer. One of his principles was the disciplined life. He opposed sexual indulgence, drinking, and purposeless living. Tolerance for all people was another of his precepts. He befriended the Jews and insisted that all religions should co-operate in making a friendly world. As a defender of liberty of faith and conscience he became a national figure. "Search for truth," he exhorted. "Oppression and falsehood must go!" This led him into political action. He taught his students to believe in the future of Bohemia. The Czech people were destined to develop and become a nation, apart from the Austrian Empire, that would stand for co-operation and progress in the life of Europe.

Professor Masaryk was elected to Parliament and soon became the recognized leader of the progressives. When the World War broke out he began four years of work for his people. He traveled from one capital to another seeking to enlist help for the Czech cause. After these months of effort the Republic of Czechoslovakia was established and he returned in 1918 as its first president. Through stormy years that saw dictators rise all around him this father of his people held to democratic ideas, insisting that his country be "a fortress of liberty in the heart of Europe and the advance guard of democracy."

"Everything depends in a democracy upon the people. They must think and work together. Institutions are not enough. We need people who are united by an ideal. Freedom of conscience and toleration must not merely be codified but realized in every domain of public life. All souls are equal; each soul belongs to itself, is independent. The main thing is to look after oneself, to control and perfect oneself, and leave others to do the same. Each one must be his own master."

Crusading tirelessly for democracy, Dr. Masaryk upheld the motto of the republic he established, "Truth will prevail." "Nothing is great if it is not true. The world demands truth and honesty. Therefore let everyone be first of all honest with himself. All honest workers are equal, and a good blacksmith is no less admirable than a good president. No one will ever know greatness who cannot begin with small things. You all want to be patriots. The very best way to do that is to be a good doctor, or teacher, or engineer. It is not enough to proclaim yourself a Czech; you must know what you have to do about it. First be the best possible kind of man yourself, then know the kind of truth the Czech tradition stands for. Your only hope of escape from complete submersion in the great nationalities pressing upon you from all sides is action—but moral action first of all. Only what is right can hope to succeed. Think out your plan, be sure it is morally true, and then act, don't dream!"

At the age of eighty-four, Dr. Masaryk was serving as the president of his country. At that time he made a statement to the dramatist, Karel Capek, "We think more of how we can lengthen life than how we can fill it. Many people are afraid of death, but they take no account of the fact that they themselves are really living only half a life, empty, loveless, without real happiness. By recognizing truth, by ordering our life morally, by loving actively, we can have a share of eternity in this life of ours, we can prolong our life not by days or years, but by eternity.

"It is good that we are trying to increase the length of a man's life, but we must do more than that; we must increase its worth. There is a dream which often comes back to me—I don't know how I come to have it, perhaps it is a recollection of some picture—I see a ship on the sea and an angel bending over it with an hour glass; and every now and then a drop runs down from the hour glass into the sea, and the angel says, 'Another minute passed away.' I always think of that dream as a warning: work, do something, while your minutes are passing."

---

4. "The Wise Man Learns to Live":

CHARLES PROTEUS STEINMETZ

It seemed an inauspicious day when another crippled Steinmetz was born in a cheap flat in the German city of Breslau. The father and his ancestors had been sadly deformed. Charles began life with the same overwhelming limitation. He could not play games and he had to guard his health. But the compensations of Providence endowed him with a brilliant mind. He won his way to the university. In spite of his abnormal body, he was respected as he proved himself to be a true scientist.

The young engineer fell under the suspicion of the police. He was involved in socialistic activities. On the threshold of completing a notable college course he was threatened with arrest. Friends hurried him off to Switzerland, where as an exile he took up mechanical engineering at the University of Zurich. A fellow student lent him money and together they emigrated to the United States.

The forlorn little cripple with his empty pocketbook and faltering English was singled out as undesirable by the immigration officers. They said, "Do you speak English?" He answered, "A few." He would have been sent back to Europe had it not been for his young friend, Asmussen, who proudly displayed his wallet of money and vouched that he would support Steinmetz until he found work. Without a penny in his pocket, with only debts to face, the diminutive engineer set out to find a job. He found it in quick order and began at twelve dollars a week in an electrical plant.

Electricity became his passion. He cared nothing for play, sleep, food, or pleasure; he was bent on discovery. His ceaseless study and diligent efforts brought him quick recognition. In 1892 the General Electric Company put Steinmetz on their staff, and the next thirty years of his life were given to them. His discoveries brought millions of dollars of income to the company and to the industrial life of the world. This tireless worker, who sacrificed family life, rest, and personal reward in his search for electrical secrets, became a popular idol of the American people. Innumerable stories were reported in the newspapers about him. He was called the "Supreme Court" in the company. One day a group of engineers were puzzled over a problem. Steinmetz was working among them, oblivious to what they were saying. They touched him on the shoulder, "If you bore a hole two inches in diameter through a rod also two inches in diameter, how much material is removed?" Steinmetz stared into space a moment and then wrote out the answer, "5.33 cubic inches."

His associates discovered that he carried the entire table

of logarithms up to one thousand in his mind and knew by memory the seven-point extension of the table. He was adept at rapid calculations in fractions and decimals. He snapped out answers between puffs on his cigar.

When Edison came to see him, Dr. Steinmetz realized that his fellow scientist was too deaf to hear what he was saying, so he reached over to Edison's knee and tapped out a message in the Morse code. A smile of amazement spread over his visitor's face. For a long time the two men telegraphed to each other in this way.

His first noteworthy discovery was in the field of magnetic losses, the law of hysteresis. Pioneer work was done with his crude equipment. During succeeding studies in the field of electricity he registered 195 patents in his name. Looking back on his career, he said, "I came to America in 1889. It seems a long way back to think where the development of electricity was at that time. It seems a long way ahead to think where it will yet be. For the age of electricity is yet to come. And it will be a great age."

The inventor was as reliable as the sun, spending long hours each day in the company laboratory, going home to continue experiments in his workshop there. He predicted the four-hour working day for American labor, but never counted the hours he put in. His laboratory was the most important part of his home. He did most of his own cooking. The favorite meal on his menu was beef steak and boiled potatoes, which he could eat day after day without variation. He gave little attention to clothes, despised buying things to wear, and went to make purchases only at the insistence of friends who were eager to keep him respectable looking.

A friend said of him, "The friendly, courteous manner toward all people, his inferiors as well as his superiors; the kindly, companionable smile that sometimes deepened into a fraternal laugh; the thoughtfulness for the good of the human race, which was so deep-seated within his heart, left with his intimate friends, and to some extent with his visitors, an impression of democratic simplicity that operated to open the heart of the 'other fellow' in friendly response. He was one of those wholly delightful people who somehow contrive to stay wholly human notwithstanding the brilliance of their renown."

"To succeed," said Steinmetz, "is to make a living at work which interests you. The work which interests you may not make you rich. What of that? The wise man learns to live. The shrewd man learns to make money. But the man who has learned to live is the happier of the two. Because his work interests him it is not work at all."

The hunchbacked wizard of electricity was well paid for his discoveries. At one time he refused a salary greater than the president of the United States was receiving. When he died, it was found that he had given his money away.

---

5. *"I Would Not Exchange
My Suffering for the
Wealth of the Indies":*

EDWARD L. TRUDEAU

KEEP the windows shut tight and don't let in the sun." These words of warning were spoken by the doctor to young Edward Trudeau, who was nursing his brother, a tuberculosis victim. He lived for weeks in the room with his brother, caring for him day and night, drinking tea to keep himself awake. There seemed to be nothing to do but give cough medicine and wait for the pale lad to die. Edward could never forget that wretched and dramatic death. From that day he caught an unquenchable sympathy for the tubercular. His vigorous body was weakened by the long ordeal and the germs of the white death began their silent work in his own lungs.

His friendship for Lottie Beare encouraged him to prepare for a profession. In 1868 he became a student in the College of Physicians and Surgeons. His friends at the club were so sceptical about his physical stamina that one of them offered a bet of five thousand dollars that Trudeau would never graduate. And no one could be found to take the wager. Tuberculosis became active before he graduated, but he was able to complete his hospital service. With the threat of impending breakdown, the young doctor married and started practice.

A few months later medical examiners told him that he had pulmonary consumption and that it was absolutely fatal. He came out of the doctor's office stunned. The sun was shining, but the world had suddenly grown dark. He was afflicted with the most fatal of diseases! He had seen its horrors in his brother. Was he ready to die? How would he tell his wife?

No treatment was considered effective. He tried exercise and grew worse. A friend took him to the Adirondack Mountains, carrying him on a mattress in a wagon to a hunting lodge. The proprietor picked him up in his arms and carried him to a room. "Why, doctor," he said, "You don't weigh no more than a dried lamb-skin!"

The rest of his life he was to remain in exile in these mountains. When he was free from fever, he would go hunting. Sometimes the guides had to move him with poles tied to a rocking chair and set him down beside a deer run. In the winter they were cut off from civilization, sixty miles from a railway station. The doctor learned the Morse code and talked with the Plattsburg operator at night to pass the time and to keep contact with the world. In 1876 his family came to join him where he battled for thirty-nine years to hold the white plague in check and to create the first tuberculosis institutions in America, the Adirondack Cottage Sanitarium and the Saranac Laboratory for the Study of Tuberculosis.

His friends, the hunting guides, contributed the land, some sixteen acres, and he built the first cottages that were to become a haven for consumptives. He was the doctor, the entire staff, and was forced to make a living for himself and expenses for his institution through practice among the summer residents. It was a new experiment, and single handed he had to win support to try out his untested ideas.

"The grounds were a rough hillside covered with scant grass, through which everywhere jutted boulders of varying sizes, a few rising four or five feet above the ground." He wrote, "Not a sidewalk, not a path anywhere! The buildings, a small rough-board and shingle barn, one unpainted cottage! The patients, two frail, ill-clad factory girls! The staff, a farmer, his wife and two daughters—all this humble agglomeration situated in an unbroken forest forty-two miles from the nearest railroad! Truly, I must have been an optimist by nature!"

In a few years there was a complete village of cottages and buildings, with barns and farms, a nurses' home and training school, a library, church, laboratory, recreational center, workshop, and many acres of forest.

Dr. Trudeau learned that Koch of Germany had isolated the tuberculosis germ. He went to New York to Dr. Prudden's laboratory to learn to use the microscope in order that he might master the technique himself. He found how to capture the bacillus and began his own researches. The tiny laboratory in which he made his first experiments was burned in 1893 while he was seriously ill in New York City. Dr. Prudden came to present him with a new microscope, while other friends built a stone laboratory for him at Saranac.

The sanitarium was built and paid for in twenty years. The doctor set as his goal an endowment of $50,000, but he saw it go beyond $600,000. In 1895 a committee from the Massachusetts legislature came to visit his institution. They returned home to found the first state sanitarium for incipient tuberculosis in the United States.

His efforts at money raising were a serious drain on his energy and many times he broke down. A year would seldom pass without acute suffering as death hovered near him. He collapsed while trying to read a paper in Baltimore before the Climatological Association. Weak and feverish, he was able to give the presidential address in 1910 before the Congress of American Physicians and Surgeons.

His daughter, Chatte, died with tuberculosis, contracting it suddenly while she was in a girls' school. She was laid to rest beside her baby brother in the little church yard at Saranac. A son, Ned, who was a physician, died with pneumonia. The people of the country loved the handsome young man, and they made the preparations for his funeral and paid all the bills. The heart-broken doctor and his wife learned in their tribulations what a wide circle of friends had been created because of their heroic devotion.

"When I thought I had come to the end, it proved but the turn in the road," he confessed. "I went to the mountains to die—I found there the beginning of a new life. . . . As I look back on my life, tuberculosis looms up as an ever-present and relentless foe. It robbed me of my dear ones, and brought me the first great sorrows of my life. It shattered my health when I was young and strong, and relegated me to this remote region where ever since I have witnessed its withering blight laid on those about me. Yet the struggle with tuberculosis has brought me experiences and left me recollections which I never would have known otherwise, and which I would not exchange for the wealth of the Indies!"

Shortly before his death the heroic doctor spoke of his favorite statue, "Gloria Victis," which shows a wounded gladiator who is lifted up by the wings of victory. "It typifies," he said, "many victories I have seen won in Saranac Lake by those whom I had learned to love; the victory of the spirit over the body; the victories that demand acquiescence in worldly failure; and in the supreme sacrifice of life itself as a part of their achievement; the victory of the Nazarene, which ever speaks its great message to the ages."

----

6. *Among the Humblest of Created Things:*

JEAN HENRI FABRE

THE LITTLE French village buzzed with excitement. The Minister of Public Instruction was visiting the schools, and he asked to be escorted to the humble home of Jean Henri Fabre, who was said to know more about insects than anyone in France. Fabre had no modern laboratory and no white-coated assistants to help him in his discoveries or in the writing of his books. He lived in a modest country home with scarcely enough money to buy food for his family, carrying on his studies of nature in the fields and woods.

The Minister of Public Instruction found Fabre in his overalls, with sleeves rolled up, and his hands red with chemical dye. The naturalist hid his "lobster claws" behind his back and apologized for his appearance. The Minister complimented him on being such an ardent worker and said, "I will help you. What do you want for your laboratory?"

"Why nothing, M. le Ministre, nothing," replied Fabre. "With a little application, the equipment I have is ample."

"What, nothing! You are unique there! The others overwhelm me with requests; their laboratories are never well enough supplied. And you, poor as you are, refuse my offer!"

Fabre told the Minister how he learned to know the insect world. On hands and knees he spent hours in the burning sun studying the wasps in their burrows, in watching beetles in the fields or observing ants in the grass. He would sit sometimes for an entire day with 'eyes focused on a little section of his own land, patiently observing the behavior of the insects that were not even seen by his neighbors. He would not waste time to look at the clock. His insatiable curiosity kept his eyes fastened on the little creatures in the grass. Other features were ruled out of his mind. For him nothing existed except the subject of his study. He concentrated on his task until the sun went down and he was forced to go home.

Oftentimes people would pass by his house in the morning and see him seated by his doorstep looking at the grass blades. At noon and at night, as they returned from their work, they found him still engaged in this strange form of activity. They would tap their heads and say, "Poor old fellow, how queer he is!" They considered him childlike because he was able to forget his meals and the clock and to concentrate on some aspect of nature's life.

But it was because he had the gift of disengaging himself from the petty facts of life that he was able to discover the uncommon facts and make them known to the world.

Through concentration Fabre made his way as a constant visitor into a realm that was unexplored by his fellowmen, and became the authoritative interpreter of its mysteries.

Intent on his studies, "his heart would beat with emotion, the sweat drip from his brow to the soil, making mortar of the dust" and he would "pass hours of oblivion in the happiness of learning." He went forth in the red dawn when spiders clung waiting below their nets, "which the tears of night have changed into chaplets of dewdrops, whose magic jewelry was sparkling in the sun," to watch the resurrection of the silkworm moth, "in order not to lose the moment when the nymph bursts her swaddling bands," or to watch the wing of the locust sprouting from its sheath, an "extraordinary anatomy in process of formation." He studied by night the Cione constructing a capsule of goldbeater's skin or the Processional caterpillars moving head to tail along their path.

He would take his findings to the walnut table "spotted with ink and scarred with knife-cuts, just big enough to hold the inkstand, a halfpenny bottle, and his open notebook." The first entries were in his notebooks. Later he made a more perfect copy, patiently revising. Most of his writing was done between the ages of sixty and ninety. Book after book was painstakingly created. "The more I go forward," he wrote, "the more clearly I see that I have struck my pick into an inexhaustible vein, well worthy of being exploited."

At eighty he said, "As though I had a long future before me, I continue indefatigably my researches into the lives of these little creatures. . . . The outer world scarcely tempts me at all; surrounded by my little family, it is enough for me to go into the woods from time to time, to listen to the fluting of the blackbirds. . . . Away with repose! For him who would spend his life properly there is nothing like work."

"He attained fame while seeking nothing but truth: and what a truth— 1e truth concealed in the humblest of created things!' When he was ninety a friend came to tell him that they were raising money to erect a statue of him in a nearby spot.

"Well, well!" he said. "I shall see myself, but shall I recognize myself? I've had so little time for looking at myself!"

"What inscription do you prefer on the statue?"

"One word: Labor!"

---

7. The Light that Has Not Failed:

CLARENCE HAWKES

WHEN he was ten years old he fell on a stone wall in the pasture lot and the resulting infection caused his left leg to be amputated at the hip. Three years later, while hunting woodcock, his father's gun exploded and the boy's eyes were blinded. The suffering of five operations over a period of two years did not release Clarence Hawkes from his dark world. He went to Perkins Institute for the blind and, having completed his education, struggled to make a living by lecturing and writing poetry. His love for the outdoors led him to nature stories and here he won his reputation.

I once asked America's blind naturalist, who at the age of sixty-six, is the author of fifty books, how he kept his intimate knowledge of nature. "It is a matter of study and cultivation," he answered. "There were only thirteen years in which I saw the earth and the sky, but I had lived much of my life outdoors up to that point. As a boy I stored up on photographic plates within my mind many thousands of pictures of brooks and woods, birds and flowers. They were developed in the dark room of my soul and still remain clear and beautiful. For nearly five years after I began to write I consulted very few books. I wrote from my own store of information. Later I began a careful study of the animals I wanted to describe. I read five years about the beaver before I wrote my story, *Shaggycoat*.

"In 1912, I published a book, *Piebald, King of Bronchos*. It was the story of a wild horse, with the scenes laid in Arizona and Nevada. It is not generally known, but there are more wild horses in the state of Nevada than there are people. About a month after the book appeared, I received a letter from a man who said that he had spent many years in Arizona, in the cattle business. He added that my book was the best description of the Arizona desert he had ever read; he wanted to know where I lived in Arizona. I had never been in the state," he chuckled.

"In 1912, I arranged with my publisher to write a book on Uncle Sam's reindeer herd in Alaska. I had never seen that country, but this did not worry me. I have always claimed that all things belong to the man with imagination, provided he can acquire enough scientific knowledge to strike a balance.

"It happened at this time that a brother-in-law who had spent two years in Alaska was visiting me, and he said he would tell me all about Alaska. So we sat down to talk it over. I began by asking him just where the Yukon River rose. He did not know exactly, but could guess at it. I asked him how broad this river was at Circle City. He was not sure. I then asked him how far it was navigable, and he was not certain. His answers to my questions about the fauna and flora of the country were equally indefinite, and he finally decided that he had not observed very much in Alaska, and what he saw he did not remember. I find this to be true of nearly everyone. Half of the world do not see things, and those who do, fail to remember what they have seen.

"I told my friend that if he would give me some time, I would answer questions about Alaska. In the meantime, I secured a good map and several scientific books on the flora and fauna of the country. I also sent to Washington and secured all of Shelden Jackson's reports on the reindeer herd in Alaska. He had been a missionary in that country and instrumental in bringing the reindeer from Finland in the revenue cutter, 'Bear,' to Alaska.

"For an hour at our next meeting, I was able to answer all of my friend's questions and make him see the country more clearly than he ever had with his own eyes."

Mr. Hawkes is a sturdy man, browned by his hours in the sun. He talks in an easy way, with a genial manner and good humor.

"In 1927, I decided to write a book on the cattle industry in the United States, laying the scene in Wyoming, and dealing with the subject exhaustively," he continued.

"I went to Forbes Library in Northampton and returned home with ten volumes on Wyoming and the cattle industry. I had for a reader this time an eighth-grade grammar school girl who did all my reading in preparation for this book and also took all my notes. In three weeks' time I was ready to write the volume.

"When it finally appeared, several of the reviews said, 'Mr. Hawkes certainly does know his West.' I have never been west of Hobart College in New York State!"

My host explained how blindness made it evident to him that it was his work in life to teach other people how to see.

99

He has not only made a living through his books but has won an audience of 3,000,000 young people around the world. He has taught them to see beauty, to protect natural life and to share his ideals. He said, "I have worked hard, and anyone else can do what I have done. I have worn out nine typewriters in my literary toils. You ask me if there is more joy than sorrow in life. For me there is more joy than tragedy. I can still say that my blindness has been a way of discipline that has brought me into a bigger life. It has meant hardship. But if I had not lost my eyesight I should probably be an unknown farmer today, following a plow in the potato fields of Western Massachusetts, and should never have found my work of teaching others to see.

"I believe that there is a guiding purpose in life. Everyone who grows quiet in the presence of the natural world knows that there is some creative plan. Most of my inspiration comes to me through the realm of nature. In the winter I am shut up in the house a good deal. When spring comes I rejoice to be free in the open air again. After four or five days out on my lawn with flowers and birds, I begin to feel a new source of vitality flowing from mother earth into my veins. And in my writing I depend on direct inspiration from these energies that are bigger than man. I might as well lay down my pen if the muse is not working and quit for the day. Beauty is all about us if we but open our lives to it!"

We walked out into his garden on the old Hadley green. "The best service I have done for the world was the translation of my autobiography, *Hitting the Dark Trail,* into French!" he explained. "Eugene Brieux, the French dramatist, had it printed in raised print. It was given to five thousand blind poilu who lost their sight in the World War."

The scent of lilacs was in the early summer air.

"But how can you know that a scarlet tanager is bathing there in the stone bath?" I was puzzled by his wizard-like knowledge of our surroundings. "And you really identified thirty-five different birds the week you spent in my Cape Cod house?"

He laughed heartily. "Why, yes. They tell me I can catch uncommon shadows on a winter day when the world is snow-covered and see tints in the clouds that very few identify. I don't know just how it is done. . . . I love to sit in a row boat with ripples on the gleaming lake lapping the sides of my craft while the hermit thrush solos for me and I breathe the peace of the silent woods about me. In this way I have found solace to bear the affliction that has been mine for over half a century!"

---

8. His Reward Was Hostility:

SUN YAT SEN

THE YOUNG men will be beheaded!" thundered the chief magistrate of the Canton *yamen*. "The Manchu government will tolerate no revolt!" It was the year 1895. Five out of the six revolutionists who had conspired to turn China into a republic were captured in a few hours' time and their heads cut off. The sixth escaped. He was a doctor of medicine, age 29, and his name was Sun Yat Sen.

Dr. Sun had gone from his boyhood home in South China to study in Hawaii. He was trained by Western doctors to appreciate science and new methods. Eager to awaken his country, he believed the only way to do it was to overthrow the corrupt Manchu government and set up a republic.

The young radical fled to Japan. Here he cut off his cue, showing that he renounced the authority of the Manchu rulers, put on European clothes, and sought to pass as a Japanese. He made his way to Hawaii, where he had many friends, and then to the United States and England, where he tried to gain support for his revolutionary program. He was captured by Chinese royalists in London and imprisoned in the Chinese Legation.

The Chinese minister planned to place him on a ship at night and send him back for execution in China. For seven days no one knew of his imprisonment. He threw messages out the window hoping that they might be picked up and reach friends. The window was boarded up. "In those days of suffering, I only beat out my heart and repented and earnestly prayed," he explained. "For six or seven days I prayed incessantly day and night. On the seventh day I felt suddenly comforted. I was absolutely without fear. I never made any attempt to put myself in that state. This was the result of prayer." An English servant had accepted his bribe and carried a note to Dr. James Cantlie. In a few hours his majesty's police surrounded the legation, waiting for the proposed flight to the ship that was to carry him to his death. The Chinese Minister was forced to surrender the revolutionist. The story of his London captivity made him a world hero. He became the symbol of China's struggle for progress.

For years Dr. Sun traveled about the world, from country to country, fleeing from spies and enemies, trying to educate foreigners to appreciate China's problems and to develop friends among the Chinese in foreign lands. In these travels he suffered hardship and danger that would have broken an ordinary man, but he held on resolutely to his program for thirty stormy years.

In 1904 his attempted revolution in Canton failed. Disguised as a woman coolie he got away in a sampan, with a price of $750,000 on his head. Friends pleaded with him to give up these daring struggles and to settle down and practise medicine. He laid plans for three more years, and in 1907 made another desperate effort to begin the revolution. This time he was almost captured. Exchanging clothes with a beggar, he climbed aboard a junk and escaped. Associates told him that the time was not ripe for his proposed changes; he should wait twenty-five years. But the invincible reformer set out on another tour of the nations to get new support.

In 1911 the long-waited revolution came, while he was abroad. He hurried back to China and was proclaimed the first president. But he did not remain president long. The differences between the north and the south and the maze of problems that arose led him to resign in favor of another leader. The progress of the republic was slow. The country was vast, the people were illiterate, means of transportation were lacking, and there were many factions to be overcome.

From 1911 until the day he died in 1925, Sun Yat Sen never gave up the battle for his ideals. Corrupt presidents and vicious war lords stood in the way of his program, but he kept working with all his strength, writing books, lecturing, serving in government offices, striving to achieve the reforms necessary for a new China. The "Father of the Chinese Republic" came to realize how long it would take to bring his program to realization. It would require years of effort, thousands of intelligent leaders, and millions of dollars.

Worn out by years of pioneering, Dr. Sun died in Peiping, leaving this manifesto for his followers: "For forty years, I have labored unceasingly for the cause of my countrymen's Revolution, the aim of which is to secure Liberty and Equality in China. The experience accumulated during these forty years profoundly convinces me of the fact that, in order to accomplish this aim, it is absolutely necessary to awaken the multitudinous people, and to unite with those races of the world, which treat us as equals, to strive together. At present the Revolution is not a complete success. It behooves my fellow worker to follow the principles which I have set forth in my published works, so that the aim may be completely achieved."

Sun's idealism met continuous rebuffs. He made a mistake in believing that the Chinese people were ready for a republic when they possessed no unity or solidarity. He trusted his fellow men, failing to appreciate the chicanery and corruption of Chinese officialdom. But he died with words on his lips that have become the driving force of a new China. From the spark of his courage a flame has been set burning which may yet lighten the largest republic in world history.

A few weeks after his death, I climbed one day to the Temple of the Azure Clouds outside Peiping where his body had been temporarily laid at rest. A group of school boys were visiting the ancient Buddhist shrine on a holiday excursion. We asked them if they knew who Dr. Sun was. They looked at us in amazement and exclaimed, "Why, he is the father of our country! We have come to pledge our lives to follow him!"

Since that time the government has erected a magnificent tomb built on a hillside near the new capital of Nanking. Amid a grove of ancient trees this mausoleum created after the best Chinese tradition has become the final resting place of the founder and first president of the republic of China. And every day in the year pilgrims from many provinces and nations climb the imposing flight of steps to pay homage to a man who held fast to faith in the face of hostility.

IV

THEY WON TRIUMPHANT FAITH

1. Voluntary Poverty:

MURIEL LESTER

I HAVE been living in hell, not paradise," the young lady of nineteen reasoned to herself. It was at a factory girls' party. She was meeting for the first time with people from the slums. Suddenly she felt an overwhelming contempt for the sham of her life spent in a wealthy, sheltered home.

For thirty years Muriel Lester has been living in the East Side of London among the forgotten people she discovered at that party. This "Jane Addams of England" is a little woman who wears severely plain clothes, but her radiant face and quiet, penetrating words give evidence of dynamic personality. With the money left by their father, Muriel and her sister, Doris, built in memory of their brother, who lost his life in the World War, an institution called Kingsley Hall. This remarkable place is a center of fellowship in the Bow district of East London, where the problems of congested slum life abound.

I made my first visit to Kingsley Hall on a warm August evening. For blocks around, children were playing on the streets, dogs were barking, cinema signs blazed their cheap allurements, and raucous music came from public houses. Within the little chapel where Muriel Lester presided, a group of about one hundred comrades were worshiping in the presence of God. When the simple but impressive service was ended, we retired to the social rooms to talk out our ideas. There were cockneys, students, clerks, housewives—all keenly alert to the world and its problems. Talking with one of the girls who had gone through the two years of discipline and had been admitted into the fellowship, I remarked, "There seems to be something real about your group here." She answered, "Yes, there is somethin' real in Kingsley Hall or it never would get hold of us girls who were raised in the dance halls of Bow!"

While making cocoa in the little kitchen, Miss Lester told me why she had chosen to live in the Bow. "We came here to try to develop a religion that would work in modern life. We were tired of hearing people say, 'there is nothing we can do to right the wrongs of politics, industry, and international relations.' We came here because we believed the first need was to keep in close touch with God. It is easier to remember God in a place like this than in the more prosperous sections of the city. People are wiser here. They do not run about from apartment to apartment; do not think so much of luxury and pleasure. Like the peasants of ancient times, they attach themselves to a place and learn to meet life with courage. We have put our first emphasis on God. Prayer gives us our guidance. It helps us to think creatively, it stretches the imagination. It helps us to see people, not as they are, but as they ought to be. It gives us the wisdom to serve others.

"Our training in meditation convinced us that we must begin to live in the streets of London as Jesus lived in Galilee. We determined to serve as he served, without distinction between class, nation, or race. We knew we must do everything in our power to avert war. During the World War we refused to hate the Germans, although we were called cowards and traitors by some of our neighbors. We decided to enter a life of voluntary poverty in order to share life with our comrades. Those who come into our fellowship go through the discipline. We live together, do our own cooking and scrubbing. We pray together, and carry on the worship and service program of Kingsley Hall. Every one has seven shillings a week and a little cubicle on the flat roof for his room." She spoke enthusiastically.

"For many years I have held a conviction that wisdom abides in the East End of London. Ever since I first came to Bow I have been learning from its inhabitants; my education is not by any means complete nor have I yet attained their high standard of courage and endurance. During these years several hundreds of young people have come to live with us here at Kingsley Hall or Children's House. They have come—men, women, and girls—direct from school, after completing their university course, and in middle age, from country and city, from Australia and America, from Ceylon and Switzerland. Most of them found peace and learned wisdom from our neighbors here.

"The East End is more restful than the West. Its inhabitants are not such temporary citizens as are the denizens of Mayfair. They do not flit about, coming and going, renting and letting their houses and flats. They remind one of the peasants of feudal times, attached to the soil."

Kingsley Hall came before the world in a striking way in 1932, when Mahatma Gandhi arrived with his Indian delegation for the London Conference on Indian Affairs. During the three months he spent in England, he cast his lot with the fellowship. Miss Lester's English *ashram* was modeled in a way after Gandhi's famous retreat in India.

She once made a trip to India to study his methods. There were many protestations from officialdom in the West side of the city, but at length it was arranged, and the Mahatma, who was "the best news value in the world," came to his little cell on Powys Road, Cheapside. While meeting with the high officials of the Empire, he endeared himself to the people of Bow. On his early morning walks he made a multitude of friends.

A young London cockney took me up to the flat roof to see the room where the famous Oriental had meditated and rested. I placed my hand on the spinning wheel that Gandhi left behind him in the cell, looked at one of his sandals on the floor, and thought of the hours he had spent there in prayer. The cockney friend said to me, "Oh yes, we all liked Mr. Gandhi. 'E got along famous with us people 'ere. Some folks couldn't understand what 'e meant when 'e talked about prayin' and givin' up things to the poor. We could understand 'im, and we loved 'im!"

I thought of Muriel Lester's words as I went away, "If you possess superfluities while your brothers lack necessities you are possessing the goods of others." For this reason she refuses to eat cake at tea, saying, "For the sake of my comrades in London, I make this little sacrifice. . . .

"If you are engaged in the big work of spreading God's love in the world, you cannot fuss about your own little self or what you feel someone else feels. You are dealing with great world forces, once you have given your life to God. Your business now is to stop war, to purify the world, to get it saved from poverty and riches, to make people like each other, to comfort the sad, to wake up those who have not yet found God, to create joy and beauty wherever you go, to find God in everything and in everyone!"

2. A Gambler for God:

TOYOHIKO KAGAWA

HE IS A lunatic!" relatives and friends said as the young student turned away from his wealthy house to try out a new religion in the slums of Kobe. And Toyohiko Kagawa wondered, when he found himself in Shinkawa, the worst slum district of the great city, if he were not a fool! He had given up the family fortune; penniless and alone he was trying to educate himself. Now he had come to apply his new religion of love in Shinkawa. The smells of the filthy streets, the wretchedness of his cell-like room, and the appalling misery of the people made him sick in body and mind. The slum folks called him a lunatic too! They thought he was a rich fool; and they came to get what they could from him. They stole his money, his clothes, and even the covers from his bed. One bully knocked him unconscious and broke off his front teeth. He was threatened with guns and knives.

One day a beggar came to him and said, "Give me your shirt; if you oppose me you are not a Christian!" He gave him the shirt. The next day he demanded Kagawa's coat and trousers, and he gave them also. All he had left was a woman's kimono that a destitute old lady had given him. It was ragged and it was lined with red (only women wear red-lined kimonos), and he was forced to wear that garment to theological seminary! A drunkard smashed all the furniture in his austere, one-room home, seized the young idealist by the throat, and kicked him in the stomach with his clogs.

His neighbors were thieves, drunkards, murderers, prostitutes, and morons. The frail student cared for these people when they were sick, went without proper food and clothing as he tried to alleviate their suffering, and pawned his clothes to buy them bowls of rice. Sharing his bed with a street urchin, he contracted trachoma and soon lost the vision of one eye. He buried the bodies of those who died with contagious diseases, paid funeral expenses for cast-off babies, and nursed lepers and the tubercular. While serving these human derelicts, he struggled to show them how they could improve their lot. He tried to carry on a program of social service and pay his expenses at theological school. The strain was so heavy that he collapsed with tuberculosis.

"He will die in a year," the doctor said as he sent Kagawa from the slums to the seashore. "If it is so," the young hero said, "I will make every day count." He found strength to write his novel, *Before the Dawn,* which sold a quarter of a million copies and made him a literary hero. Enticing jobs were offered him, but he said "No." Back to the slums he went! "I know a family of gamblers," he wrote. "When they lose, they send one of their sons to run to the pawn shop and pawn his coat to get money. This boy becomes naked, and loses everything for gambling. Because I lived in the slums I have become a gambler for God. I want to pawn everything for Christ!"

Kagawa's body has been battered by disease, but his soul remains unconquered. He is half blind, he has suffered for years with tuberculosis, his heart and his kidneys have been weakened by many ailments. I once marveled at his exuberance and strength. He said to me, "Doctors gave me up years ago. It is faith in God that has kept me going. I am amazed at the strength that comes to me when I pray and trust God!"

While visiting the United States, Dr. Kagawa spoke for two hours to a group of American friends on his faith in God, which has brought him illumination and healing in times of despair when blindness threatened, hunger and imprisonment terrified him, and death hovered close. His testimony convinced us that a contemporary saint was before us, a prophet who worked miracles among the sordid realities of the twentieth century, a mystic who laughed at the impossible. Associated with him for hours at a time in automobile, hotel, and public meetings, I have not yet seen him lose his serenity, register malice, or show any concern over the commonplace things of the world.

The author of more than sixty books, he has devoted all his royalties to establishing three settlements among the slum people in Kobe, Osaka, and Tokyo. He has given away thousands of dollars while large groups of co-workers, who assist him in his vast program for world peace, public health, agricultural progress, and industrial reform, depend upon him for their income. He and his family of four make personal sacrifices to carry on this huge undertaking.

"With faith in God's guidance I will run through the dark to the uttermost of my strength!" He exclaims, "My life will be victory crowned!" Tireless and serene, he is unafraid of worry or pain. "If one lives for a long time immersed in God's grace there stretches across one's inner soul a calm which nothing can destroy. When, guarded by five officers of the law, I was thrown into prison pending trial, when marching with a mob of 15,000 people along a street seething with riot, when threatened with daggers in the hands of desperadoes, the jewel of peace, hidden away in my soul, was in no wise disturbed. When in an automobile crash the city tram rumbled on over me, that inner peace was still maintained. Even when a chronic eye disease threatened to rob me of my sight I experienced no swells on the calm sea of my soul. Even I myself stand amazed at this calm!"

Kagawa's peace is disturbed only by one thing, the suffering of his fellowmen: "Oh, my soul! My soul!" he cries. "Do you hear God's pain-pitched cry as He suffers because of the world's sore distress? God dwells among the lowliest of men. He sits on the dust heap among the prison convicts. With the juvenile delinquents He stands at the door, begging bread. He throngs with the beggars at the place of alms. He is among the sick. He stands in line with the unemployed. Therefore, let him who would meet God visit the prison cell before going to the temple. Before he goes to church let him visit the hospital. Before he reads the Bible let him help the beggar standing at his door!"

He is a gambler for God! He loses himself in striving to redeem humanity!

"I want to live! I want to conquer!

"I want to conquer illness, ignorance, evil, ugliness, apostasy.

"I want to be fully awake to Reality.

"Fulness of life for me will bring fulness of life to the Race.

"Fulness of life for the Race will mean fulness of life for the Universe.

"The Universe has a purpose for me.

"The Universe is awakening in me.

"Thus let me lay hold of Life,

"And glorify this seemingly sordid civilization,

"And push it upward!"

-----

3. Up the Mountain Path:

SADHU SUNDAR SINGH

How I STUDIED all our sacred books! How I strove for peace and rest of soul! I did good works: I did all that could lead on to peace! But I did not find it; for I could not achieve it for myself." The young Sikh aristocrat was heartbroken at the age of fourteen. His mother had died; he had no belief to comfort him. After a year of further searching he burned the New Testament in the courtyard of his home before a group of friends to show his contempt for its creeds.

Soon after his fifteenth year, Sundar Singh decided to take his own life. He would put his head on the track as the five o'clock morning train went by. If there were no satisfaction in this life, perhaps there would be in the next. He got up early and prayed; and suddenly his room was filled with light. In his vision he saw the figure of Christ, who commanded him to believe in the worthwhileness of life and in his power to make it worthwhile for others.

He ran to his father. "I have become a Christian," he cried. "Go lie down and sleep," his father returned. "Why, only a short time ago you burnt the Bible; and now you say you are a Christian!"

The tall, handsome young man was determined. No persuasion could alter his purpose to serve the masses of India. He was publicly excluded from the family and from the Sikh religion. He was driven from the house and spent his first night in cold weather under a tree. It was an unhappy beginning of his new career. The forlorn lad reasoned to himself: "Yesterday and before that I used to live in the midst of luxury at my home; but now I am shivering here, hungry, thirsty, without shelter, with no warm clothes and no food."

He put on the robes of a Sadhu. Penniless, homeless, he began his wanderings among the poor, the outcasts, the lepers. He held to his purpose for years. He walked thousands of miles over burning sands and mountain paths, searching out the orphans, fighting for uplift of the untouchables. He traveled about the world to tell people about the life of love that God demanded. His lectures and books brought acclaim. But he turned away from Europe and

America with disappointment. He could not bear to see the luxury of the West, when millions in India were starving. He disliked the noise and rush of the Occident. "God is always quiet," he said. "He never makes a noise. His voice is a still, small voice."

He hurried back to India seeking the most difficult challenge he could find. He made his way over the Himalaya Mountains into Tibet. Tibet fascinated him; it was isolated, inaccessible, undeveloped. He yielded often during his lifetime to the lure of its unexplored highlands, and climbed up mountain passes 19,000 feet high. He made his way through wind and snow, swam icy rivers, lived for weeks on barley grain, suffered fever and cold that he might bring new life to the people there.

The Lama priests of Tibet impressed him and won his sympathy. "They shut themselves up," he said, "in a dark cell. Some remain in this condition for a number of years. Some stay in darkness for their whole lives. They never see the sun and never come out. They sit inside and turn a prayer wheel. Thus they live, just as if they were in the grave. On one side of their dark cells they make a small hole through which people put food for them to eat. From these hermits I learned a lesson. For these people go through all this suffering to gain that which is nothing at all. They do it to reach Nirvana, which holds out no prospect of a future life of joy, but only leads to the extermination of life and spirit and all desire. This is their idea of salvation. How much more ought we to serve Christ and lay hold on eternal life and in his name joyfully take up the cross of service to others!"

Sadhu Sundar Singh returned from these perilous journeys to work among the lepers, to nurse the sick and teach the illiterate, to aid his American fellow-worker, Samuel Stokes, in collecting crippled and blind boys to take to a summer camp in the mountains. Ragged old men would bow before him as he went through village streets; he would lift them up and talk in his kindly way to them. He used Christ's method in his speaking, creating his own parables from nature and Indian life. He became the St. Francis of India.

In the spring of 1929 he made his last pilgrimage to Tibet. Friends had warned him and entreated him not to go. His eyesight was impaired; his lungs were affected; his heart had been overtaxed. The magnificent physique of the stalwart, dark aristocrat had been broken by the fierce abandonment demanded by the flame within.

He has never returned from that journey. He must have died somewhere in the wilds of the inaccessible mountains. Although sick and weary, he bade farewell to his comrades in the valley with a song on his lips. It was his last song, but he made it a hymn of victory.

---

4. "Prove Your Worth":
JAMES E. K. AGGREY

THE SON of an African chieftain, James Aggrey, at fifteen, was in charge of a boy's school of forty students, and at twenty-three the headmaster of a large institution. He migrated to the United States to complete his education and serve as professor in Livingstone College in North Carolina. He carried on studies in education at Columbia University, and when free from teaching duties learned shorthand, printing, farming, osteopathy, and law. Eager to help the illiterate, desperately poor Negroes around him, he became the minister of two country churches.

"You should be doing religion and living education," he wrote in his vivid way. "I will explain what I mean by doing religion. I went to the Mission. I finished standard seven and four years in High School. I taught for nine years, then I went to America and graduated from college. I went to the country to preach. I could quote Hebrew, Greek and Latin, but what did my people care about that? My people were poor, living eight or ten in one room. They wanted something, and I failed as everyone else ought to fail who preaches that kind of theology. I was in an airplane, and I had to come down. I started preaching on, 'Give ye them to eat'—preaching chickens, goats, something to eat, something to wear. I had a sermon on the angels. I told them that mosquitoes, flies and so on were messengers from God. Mosquitoes come to say, 'There is death round here; I am talking to you; don't you hear me? As long as you don't hear it, the swamp stays and will give you disease. Clean it.' Then they sing another song, 'Let thy servant depart in peace.' After church we had a meeting to appoint a look-out committee. They found an old lady who had no wood at all. They said, 'She won't come to church.' I detailed about ten to get wood and help people, and they began to come to church.

"The kind of Christianity we have to practise is to go round helping people, and then when you pray they will say, 'Amen.' There is too much talking; talking is cheap, unless you want to use a long-distance telephone, then you have to pay the price."

The learned professor knew how to recreate lives. He organized a co-operative to buy fertilizer and new stock.

"I told my people what the land needed to enrich it; told them to put in lime and so on, and they were able to pay a little better. Mr. Thomas Miller, the man who looked after my salary, owed a thousand pounds. I said to my people,

'Let us go to work to raise to pay it,' and they did. Then I preached on such texts as, 'A sower went forth to sow,' 'Except a corn of wheat fall into the ground and die it abideth alone. . . .' I began to tell the people how to feed their children. So many are lost through ignorance of the laws of nature—some of these may have been destined to be Luthers and Booker Washingtons. If you knew how to cook, you could change the world!"

He kept hammering away on common sense. Prove your worth! Make yourself honored by doing something indispensable.

"In an American village the Blacks complained, once to me that the Whites never spoke to them. I answered, 'Produce something that is useful to Whites, and they will talk to you. Raise chickens, have eggs to sell, and you will see a change.' I set myself in season and out of season, even in my sermons, to advise the raising of chickens, and soon all the Blacks had them to sell, and eggs, and the attitude of the Whites changed toward them, and they grew, some of them wealthy. You must make yourselves indispensable—that is how you can improve your condition."

The liberal governor of the African Gold Coast, Sir Gordon Guggisberg, enlisted Dr. Aggrey in the task of building a new college for Africans, the Prince of Wales College at Achimota. The word Achimota means untouchable. It was for years a hiding place for escaped slaves. On this ground, a symbol of the wrongs perpetrated upon the black race by the white man, a college was built to champion understanding and co-operation between the two races. Aggrey came back to Africa to lead in the program and to serve as its chief advocate of inter-racial good will.

"I am a debtor to all men, to all civilizations," he exclaimed, "to world-Christianity, and to all kinds of educational programs." "Men should be too busy to nurse even personal wrongs when they are working for the good of humanity. I leave my feelings at home. I am busy working for harmony."

His was a proud and highly sensitive nature. Insults hurt him; but he disciplined himself through self-mastery. When he started on a journey he would whisper, "Keep your temper and smile." This was no easy goal for an educated black man in America or Africa.

One day he was crossing Johannesburg to attend a meeting of whites and blacks where he was to act as a mediator. When he tried to board a train to go to the meeting, some white men pushed him off into the mud. He told the story with a laugh, "So I took a taxi, which the white man's committee paid for, so the joke was on him after all!" Traveling on the Pacific, he was asked to move from the dining saloon of the ship and to eat by himself. He said at the end of the voyage, "The joke was again on the white men, since they had one waiter between eleven of them, and I had him all to myself! Laughing is the way to go through life. It is the positive side of Christ's law of non-resistance. If I find a man scowling at me, I just smile back. He scowls again and I smile back. He scowls again and I smile. I don't often find anyone scowling a third time."

Good humor and brilliant repartee were indispensable in his conciliatory technique. A white man once said to him, "African, you are not going to heaven; only white folks are going there, for God is white and the devil is black. When you die you are going to go where the devil belongs, and we will go to heaven."

"Well, I have found out in the Bible that no white people are going to heaven, only colored folks," Aggrey answered.

"How do you know that?" asked the white man.

"Well, I discovered it in the Bible. Doesn't it say that on the last day the sheep will be on the right and that the goats will be on the left, and doesn't it say that to the goats it will be said, 'Depart ye,' and to the sheep, 'Come, ye blessed'?

"Well," asked the white man, "what does that have to do with the black folks getting into heaven?"

"What race on earth, except the black race," he said, "has anything on his head that reminds you of the wool on the sheep?"

He held that the singing habit of the Negro was destined to make a profound contribution to civilization.

"Some people took to war; we took to love; some people took to hate; we took to song; some people took to anger; we took to laughter; some people took to despair; we took to hope. 'Patrol is going to get you; the bloodhound is going to get you; you can't run as fast as the bloodhounds; what are you going to do, black man?' In the darkest part of the night when everybody else might have despaired, we looked and we sang, long before our white brothers thought of an airplane, 'Swing Low, Sweet Chariot, coming for to carry me home'."

Professor Aggrey died at the age of fifty-two, while on a visit to the United States. The Prince of Wales College had been established and was progressing; he was its recognized leader. As the conciliator, he had become one of the most noted sons of Africa. His solution of the inter-racial problem was not amalgamation or conflict, but co-operation. He spoke in parables, and one of his favorites was the story of the piano keys: "You can play a tune of sorts on the white keys, and you can play a tune of sorts on the black keys, but for harmony you must use both the black and the white."

He pointed out the same principle in another figure: "We have the quarterback and the right and left tackle, and the right and left half, and then the center and fullback. The ball must be carried over, and when it is carried over it will be not one person, not the team, but the college that won.

What I say is this: no man down, all men up—all of them, white, black, yellow, brown, all—all men up, and no man down, each of us as races making our best contribution to the life of all, for each of us has a contribution to make."

Dynamic Aggrey burnt out his life to lift his people. He left behind a ringing summons in a letter to his nephew:

"To those who have fire I give more fire and to those who have might I want to give a mightier than man's. I want to sing a song of hope to the despairing; to breathe the breath of love that will chase away all hating. I believe, my devoted nephew, that right will ultimately conquer wrong, virtue conquer vice, harmony take the place of discords."

---

5. The Blindfolded Player:

TAKEO IWAHASHI

TAKEO IWAHASHI was a student in Waseda University in his twentieth year when he lost his eyesight. After seven operations and much suffering, the doctors told him that he was to be blind the rest of his life. The young Japanese stayed in his room day after day weeping. His life seemed to be a slow suicide. He wrote:

"My daily life that had hitherto been so calm and plain began to retrograde with tempo allegro, and the dreadful abyss of death might await me at any moment. The darkness extended all over the world. Fate had purposely paved my road with briars, racking my head and pricking my feet, to exile me into a black wilderness. . . . I can believe in nothing. There can be no God. Life is darkness and fortune is ever blind."

He prepared to take his own life one New Year's eve. His mother came into the room just in time to save him. She entreated, "You must live, no matter what your condition. If you die, life is not worth living for me."

She had gone from shrine to shrine praying for his recovery. Her words proved to him that love was real. In his suffering he had complained bitterly and the whole household was upset and heartbroken. He determined to save himself and make good for the sake of his family. He learned to read Braille and found inspiration in the courage of blind leaders like Homer, the poet of Greece, Milton, the poet of England, and Faucett, who was Postmaster-general of England under Gladstone.

For the first time he read the New Testament. What impressed him most was what Christ said to his disciples when they passed a blind man. The disciples asked, "Master, who did sin, this man or his parents, that he was born blind?" Jesus answered, "Neither has this man sinned nor his parents,—but that the work of God should be manifest in him." Iwahashi felt that through his blindness he was going to be of help to the world.

He cried, "I am no longer a victim of fatalism. I have a mission in life. For me there is no other way, but to boldly adventure on Jesus' sense of mission in life. Reality that contains sorrow, failure, agony, offenses, and sufferings from illness is not the mere consequence of the past, but is even a positive preparation for a better future. Let yesterday bury yesterday! We have to save our Present out of the Past in order that our bodies may manifest the glory of God."

Iwahashi returned to the university and won his degree through the devoted help of his sister, who followed him about like a shadow, reading to him and guiding him. She gave two years of her life in this service. Impatient with the restraint of blindness, he was often impatient and despondent. Students ridiculed him for depending on a girl, but the brother and sister held to their purpose. She married Iwahashi's closest friend, Professor Jugaku, now a teacher of English literature and an authority on William Blake.

A nurse in the Kyoto University Hospital became Iwahashi's wife, and through the aid of her eyes he journeyed to Scotland and studied in the University of Edinburgh. Quakers in the Scottish city befriended the heroic young couple who won a place of high respect in the university and civic life. They returned to the homeland, where Dr. Iwahashi became professor of philosophy in the Kwansei Gakuin in Kobe. His novels and philosophic writings have made him the beloved blind philosopher of Japan.

He sums up the drama of his life in this story of two pictures. In the early days of his blindness he thought of life in terms of a painting he had seen, called "The End of the Journey." It was a dark gray canvas representing a limitless desert. In the middle of the burning sands a weary camel sank down dejected from thirst and exhaustion. To him life seemed to be "The End of the Journey," dreary and desolate. From the bottomless pit of darkness he was tortured by a ruthless doom.

After months of suffering, his discovery of God brought to mind another picture that he had once seen. It was "Hope," painted by Watts of England. The painting represented a young woman who was seated on the sphere of the earth playing a lyre, in bold relief against a blue sky. The girl was blindfolded. All the strings on the lyre were broken except one. Although blindfolded and handicapped, she played valiantly on the one remaining string her song of "Hope."

"My history is expressed by these two paintings," wrote Professor Iwahashi. "Life began anew for me when I turned

from despair to hope!   Life is to be saved only by life: spirit
settled only by spirit!"

---

6. *"Friends, Do Not Be
    Afraid of Life"*:

FEODOR MIKHAYLOVICH DOSTOEVSKY

BORN in the year 1821 in the lodge of a Moscow work house
infirmary, Feodor Dostoevsky grew up with the dregs of
society.   His childhood was bleak and lonely, and he suffered from epilepsy.   His father was a doctor in one of the
public hospitals of the city.   Feodor graduated from the
Military Engineers' School and served two years in the army.
He wasted the money that was left him by his father.   On
leaving the army, he found himself penniless.

Three times he rose to the pinnacle of success; and each
time failure pulled him down again.   At the age of twenty-
four he wrote his first book, *Poor Folk,* a story of the struggles of contemporary Russia.   He became famous overnight.
The poet Nekrassov rushed to Feodor's lodging, threw his
arms about the young writer, kissed his cheeks, and told
him that he was a leader of Russian literature.   The critic,
Belinsky, questioned the new author, "Do you yourself understand *what* you have written?"

The writer of *Poor Folk* enjoyed but a few weeks of
fame.   Other visitors came to his rooms.   They were Cossacks, and they demanded his arrest.   He was a radical, a
member of the socialist circle of Petrashevsky, who met to
talk in discontented terms about the conditions of Russia.
He was imprisoned in the fortress for eight months, charged
with participation in a conspiracy against the government.

He and his nineteen comrades were sentenced to be shot. Blindfolded, he stood one day at dawn tied to a post, awaiting the volley of the executioners. The Czar's change of sentence was read. Instead of the death before the firing squad he was condemned to eight years' penal servitude in Siberia.

For nine years he was an exile from the literary world. While serving in the convict prison at Omsk, he had only one book to read, the Bible. He was never alone with himself as he lived with all types of criminals in this "house of the dead." He passed his time in carrying bricks, grinding alabaster, and shoveling snow. At night he read his one book. When released from prison he married, but he was not happy in this relation. He passed through a spiritual crisis. He threw over the social ideas of his youth and began to think in terms of the religion of the Russian nation and of his peoples' destiny to achieve a new order. His health had been injured, his epilepsy aggravated.

He was a new man when he returned to Russia in 1859, a man who had been forgotten. But he was determined to write greater books and win new friends. With his brother he started the magazine, *Vremya,* which met with favor. His writing was received with acclaim. In a year's time he was the literary leader of the nation. Then suddenly his paper was suppressed and he faced financial ruin. For eight years he carried impossible burdens. His wife died, then his brother, Michael, and his friend, Grigoriev. He was involved in a tragic love with Mlle. Suslova, and lost heavily through gambling. He tried to shoulder the care of his brother's family. After fifteen months of heroic effort he was bankrupt.

In that year he wrote his unique book, *Memoirs from Underground.* He set to work on his great novels in a last endeavor to meet his creditors. In two years' time he completed *Crime and Punishment* and *The Gambler.* He sold the copyright to all his works for $1,500. His faithful secretary, Anna Grigorievna, became his wife in 1867, and then he was forced to leave Russia to escape his creditors.

Penniless, disheartened, suffering with epilepsy, Russia's man of genius wandered about Europe. He lived in miserable quarters, where he wrote furiously to re-establish his reputation and earn enough to ward off starvation. At night in threadbare garments he crept into some cafe or club where he could find a Russian newspaper and could dream of the country he loved. This period of suffering was the most productive in his stormy life.

Able to return to the fatherland when he was fifty-two, he served as editor of a journal and enjoyed an established income again. Political changes brought popularity to his ideals and caused his influence to grow. *The Brothers Karamazov* marked the height of his power. His address at the unveiling of the Pushkin memorial made him the hero of his people. He won them with his ecstatic words about a nobler Russia. But in a few days death came, and multitudes crowded about the tomb of their new prophet. . . .

Looking back on his tumultuous years, which seemed barren of the consolations of normal living, he wrote, "You must know that there is nothing higher and stronger and more wholesome and good for life in the future than some good memory, especially a memory of childhood and home. People talk to you a great deal about your education; but some good, sacred memory, preserved from childhood, is perhaps the best education. If a man carries many such memories with him into life, he is safe to the end of his days; and if one has only one good memory left in one's heart, even that may sometime be the means of saving us. . . . Ah, dear friends, do not be afraid of life! How good life is when one does something good and just!"

Through his sufferings the buffeted searcher clung to a faith in life and in God. "Through struggle he grew strong;

the hammer blows on the anvil of his life forged his supreme powers," comments his admirer, Stefan Zweig. "The more debilitated his body, the higher soared his faith; the greater his sufferings as a man, the easier was it for him to perceive the meaning and the need of world wide suffering. . . . 'Only by suffering can we learn to love life.' Who utters these consoling words? Dostoevsky himself, the sufferer of sufferers. His hands are still nailed to the cross of his inner contradictions, but now he kisses the cruel tree of life, and his lips are gentle as they disclose the secret to his fellow-sufferers: 'I believe we must first of all learn to love life!' "

The great characters he created won consolation through this love for humanity, and triumphed over the world's despair by becoming one with God. Father Zosima declared this philosophy in Dostoevsky's last work: "Those who curse God and curse life are really cursing themselves. If you will only love each thing, the secret of God will be revealed unto you; and in the end you will embrace the whole world in the magnitude of your love."

Perhaps some of them remembered as they tramped by his casket that this man of the people who lived in the depths and climbed to the pinnacles, to fall again and again, had won his victory: "Only by suffering can we learn to love life! . . . Friends, do not be afraid of life!"

---

7. *"The Rose Above the Mould"*:

SIR WILLIAM OSLER

THE MOST beloved physician of modern times was born in 1849 in a tiny cottage at Bond Head in the wilderness of upper Canada. His father and mother had come from England as missionaries. Bond Head was a village of two hundred people, twelve miles from a post office and fifteen miles from a doctor. Willie Osler was tied in the field near the parsonage with a rope about his waist, to the same stake as the calf. One day he fell into a bucket full of milk, his friend, the calf, peering at him with fascinated interest.

Religion dominated the home, which lacked all material luxuries. From this amazing family came three brothers who also achieved fame: one became justice of the Court of Appeal in Ontario, another the leading Queen's counsel in the Dominion, another president of the Dominion Bank of Canada.

Willie nearly broke up the grammar school in Dundee. One morning a flock of geese was found quartered in the common school, in the room below the grammar school. Another morning the desks of the older pupils were found hoisted upstairs. Willie was sent home to his reverend father. He did better at the boarding school in Barrie, where he won a prize for football kicking. While in bed with an injured shin, which had been hurt playing rugby, his favorite teacher, "Father" Johnson, taught him to use the microscope and aroused in the boy a love for science. In the Toronto Medical School he found another inspirer in Dr. James Bovell, who converted him into a zealous pathologist. A third teacher, Dr. Palmer Howard, scholarly surgeon of McGill Medical School, influenced him profoundly.

During postgraduate studies in London, Berlin, and Vienna, the young doctor made one of his significant contributions to medicine through his observation of blood platelets. He returned to McGill as professor, equipping one of the first laboratories for the microscopic study of physiology and pathology. He was a disciple of the pioneers, Koch and Virchow. During a smallpox epidemic in Montreal he took charge of the cases in the General Hospital. As pathologist, he began studies in the autopsy room as a morbid anatomist. The elaborate records he kept are proof of his industry. He printed in book form the first careful hospital record on post mortem cases.

In addition to studies of smallpox, hog cholera, and typhoid fever, he developed his love for books and book collecting. The school library was his pet. Translating foreign articles, editing a journal, founding a students' medical club, and fraternizing with fellow doctors crowded the years with activity. At thirty-five he accepted a call to the Medical School of the University of Pennsylvania. Five years later he took charge of the medical department in the new Johns Hopkins Hospital in Baltimore.

He wrote a textbook that has been used around the world, *The Principles and Practice of Medicine.* This literary activity was crowded in between hospital visits, teaching, and lecturing. A champion of preventive medicine, he took up the crusade against tuberculosis, typhoid fever, and pneumonia. He lived to see typhoid practically conquered and tuberculosis under new controls, but the last foe was to claim his own valiant life. He fought side by side with Dr. Edward Trudeau, advocating in 1891 that "fresh air and sunshine" could check the white plague.

Dr. Osler was a doctor to his own profession. They came from all over the continent to seek his advice. He went on long pilgrimages to serve fellow physicians in need. His common sense and natural optimism made him an ideal helper of the sick. In his address, *The Student Life,* he said:

"Lift up one hand to heaven and thank your stars if they have given you the proper sense to enable you to appreciate the inconceivably droll situations in which we catch our fellow creatures. . . . Hilarity and good humor, a breezy cheerfulness, a nature 'sloping towards the sunny side,' as

Lowell has it, help enormously both in the study and in the practice of medicine. . . . It is an unpardonable mistake to go about among patients with a long face."

Wit characterized his teaching: "Who serves the gods dies young—Venus, Bacchus, and Vulcan send in no bills in the seventh decade. . . . The mental kidney more often than the abdominal is the one that floats. . . . Believe nothing that you see in the newspapers—they have done more to create dissatisfaction than all other agencies. If you see anything in them that you know is true, begin to doubt it at once."

Osler knew how to utilize his time. In trains and taxis he pulled out his note book and set to work. He read quickly during spare moments. He could escape irritations as if by magic and concentrate on his program. There is a master word, he said. "The stupid man it will make bright, the bright man brilliant, and the brilliant student steady. With the magic word in your heart all things are possible, and without it all study is vanity and vexation. . . . And the master word is Work."

The lover of books was read to during his bath, and during those extra minutes over a period of years surveyed some of the classics. "Divide your attention equally between books and men," he said. "The strength of the student is to sit still—eating the heart out of a subject with pencil and notebook in hand, determined to master the details and intricacies." His favorite was *Religio Medici,* by Sir Thomas Browne.

"The practice of medicine is an art, not a trade; a calling, not a business; a calling in which your heart will be exercised equally with your head. Often the best part of your work will have nothing to do with potions and powders, but with the exercise of an influence of the strong upon the weak, of the righteous upon the wicked, the wise upon the foolish."

Religion was his ultimate refuge. "I begin each day with Christ and his prayer," he stated. "At night as I lay off my clothes I undress my soul, too, and lay aside its sins. In the presence of God I lie down to rest and to waken a free man with a new life."

In 1905 he became Regius Professor of Medicine at Oxford. An increasing love for books was satisfied by the hours he spent in the Bodleian library, where he served as curator. His collection of rare volumes grew steadily with his travels. Lectures took him throughout the English-speaking world. His influence in public health and hospitalization grew and became world wide. He fought against the mass diseases brought by the World War. But the poison generated by the conflict drove him to the consolation of books.

His son, Revere, an only child, was killed. The father had been tormented since he enlisted. " 'Fear at my heart, as at a cup, my life-blood seemed to sip.' I never saw a wounded man without thinking of Revere, and since October, since he went out, every telegram has been opened with dread." Osler became a mere shadow of his former self. He tried to carry on, revising his textbook, welcoming Canadians and Americans who found open house with him and Lady Osler at any time, but he sobbed night after night in tormenting dreams. He made his usual rounds to the homes of friends where there were little children to play with. He tried to father the wounded and broken derelicts of the war. But his wife wrote, "He grows thinner all the time; I can't have him lose another ounce of flesh, his bones will come through."

He said in public address, "Two things are clear: there must be a very different civilization or there will be no civilization at all; and the other is that neither the old religion combined with the old learning, nor both with the new science, suffice to save a nation. . . ." We must "encourage in

130

all a sense of brotherhood reaching the standard of the Good Samaritan." As president of the Inter-allied Fellowship of Medicine he tried to help medical men involved in the war. He took the lead in sending food and supplies to the starving war victims of Austria and Germany.

Bronchitis and pneumonia kept him lingering near the gateway of death for several months following his seventieth birthday celebration. He clung to his optimism, greeting the doctor with, "I had a good night, and smell the rose above the mould this morning." During paroxysms of coughing he would reach out with emaciated hand and pick up a slice of lemon. With a brave smile he tossed the peel upon the head of his wife or nurse who watched with troubled eyes by the bed. He kept writing pads under his pillow and during these last weeks of suffering wrote down detailed instructions about the disposition of his many valuable books. A memorial library named after his son was to be created in Johns Hopkins University. Other volumes were assigned to libraries in various medical centers. He laughed, "Well, it's Michael Angelo and his tomb, and Osler and his Library!"

With one of his addresses the words of a poem were found copied in his handwriting:

"For Yesterday is but a Dream
And Tomorrow is only a Vision;
But Today well lived makes
Every Yesterday a Dream of Happiness,
And every Tomorrow a Vision of Hope.
Look well therefore to this Day!
Such is the Salutation of the Dawn!"

SOURCES OF QUOTATIONS

THE SOURCES of the direct quotations included in this volume are listed below according to section and number. The author is grateful to the publishers of these books for their permission to use this material.

I

1. *Noguchi,* Gustav Eckstein, Harper and Brothers, 1931.
2. *The Saga of Fridtjof Nansen,* Jon Sorensen, translated by J. B. C. Watkins, W. W. Norton and Co., 1932.
3. *Martha Berry, The Sunday Lady of Possum Trot,* Tracy Byers, G. P. Putnam's Sons, 1932.
5. *Osborne of Sing Sing,* Frank Tannenbaum, University of North Carolina Press, 1933.
6. *Clerambault,* Romain Rolland, translated by Katherine Miller, Henry Holt and Co., 1921.
   The Death of a World, Romain Rolland, translated by Amalia de Alberti, Henry Holt and Co., 1933.
   A World in Birth, Romain Rolland, translated by Amalia de Alberti, Henry Holt and Co., 1934.
7. *Edward Wilson of the Antarctic,* George Seaver, John Murray, 1933.
8. *Eugene V. Debs,* McAlister Coleman, Greenberg, 1930.
9. *Jane Addams of Hull House,* Winifred E. Wise, Harcourt, Brace and Co., 1935.
10. *Justice Oliver Wendell Holmes,* Silas Bent, Vanguard Press, 1932.

II

1. *Life and Letters of John Galsworthy,* H. V. Marrot, Charles Scribner's Sons, 1936.
2. *Saint Peter Relates an Incident,* James Weldon Johnson, Viking Press, 1935.
   Negro Americans, What Now? James Weldon Johnson, Viking Press, 1934.
3. *Jeremiah,* Stefan Zweig, translated by Eden and Cedar Paul, Viking Press, 1929.
4. *What I Owe to Christ,* C. F. Andrews, Abingdon Press, 1932.
6. *Victories of Peace,* D. M. Gill and A. Pullen, Friendship Press, 1936.
8. *Lord Shaftesbury,* J. L. Hammond and Barbara Hammond, Harcourt, Brace and Co., 1924.
9. *Memoirs of a Revolutionist,* Peter Kropotkin, Houghton Mifflin Co., 1899.
10. *The Way to World Peace,* H. G. Wells, Ernest Benn, 1930.

III

1. *Anne Sullivan Macy, The Story Behind Helen Keller,* Nella Braddy, Doubleday, Doran and Co., 1933.
2. "A World-Famous Singer Whose Parents Were Slaves," Mary B. Mullett, *American Magazine,* June, 1925, Crowell Pub. Co.
3. *President Masaryk Tells His Story,* Karel Capek, Allen and Unwin, 1934.
   Masaryk, Nation Builder, Donald Lowrie, Association Press, 1930.
4. *Charles Proteus Steinmetz,* John W. Hammond, D. Appleton-Century Co., 1924.
5. *An Autobiography,* E. L. Trudeau, Lea and Febiger.
6. *The Life of Jean Henri Fabre,* Abbe Augustin Fabre, Dodd, Mead and Co., 1921.
   Fabre, Poet of Science, C. V. Legros, D. Appleton-Century Co., 1913.

7. *The Light that Did Not Fail,* Clarence Hawkes, Chapman and Grimes, 1935.
8. *Sun Yat Sen,* Henry B. Restarick, Yale University Press, 1931.

IV

2. *Kagawa,* William Axling, Harper and Brothers, 1932.
3. *Sadhu Sundar Singh,* Charles F. Andrews, Harper and Brothers, 1934.
4. *Aggrey of Africa,* Edwin W. Smith, Harper and Brothers, 1929.
5. *Light From Darkness,* Takeo Iwahashi, John C. Winston Co., 1933.
6. *Three Masters,* Stefan Zweig, translated by Eden and Cedar Paul, Viking Press, 1930.
   The Brothers Karamazov, Feodor M. Dostoevsky.
7. *The Life of Sir William Osler,* Harvey Cushing, Oxford University Press, 1925.